Tempo
A Scarecrow Press Music Series on Rock, Pop, and Culture

Series Editor: Scott Calhoun

Tempo: A Scarecrow Press Music Series of Rock, Pop, and Culture offers titles that explore rock and popular music through the lens of social and cultural history, revealing the dynamic relationship between musicians, music, and their milieu. Like other major art forms, rock and pop music comment on their cultural, political, and even economic situation, reflecting the technological advances, psychological concerns, religious feelings, and artistic trends of their times. Contributions to the Tempo series are the ideal introduction to major pop and rock artists and genres.

Bon Jovi: America's Ultimate Band, by Margaret Olson, 2013.

Ska: The Rhythm of Liberation, by Heather Augustyn, 2013.

Ska

The Rhythm of Liberation

Heather Augustyn

THE SCARECROW PRESS, INC.
Lanham • Toronto • Plymouth, UK
2013

Published by Scarecrow Press, Inc.
A wholly owned subsidiary of The Rowman & Littlefield Publishing Group, Inc.
4501 Forbes Boulevard, Suite 200, Lanham, Maryland 20706
http://www.scarecrowpress.com

Estover Road, Plymouth PL6 7PY, United Kingdom

British Library Cataloguing in Publication Information Available

Library of Congress Cataloging-in-Publication Data

Augustyn, Heather, 1972-
Ska : the rhythm of liberation / Heather Augustyn. pages ; cm. -- (Tempo: a Scarecrow Press music series on rock, pop, and culture)
Includes bibliographical references and index.
ISBN 978-0-8108-8449-6 (cloth : alk. paper) -- ISBN 978-0-8108-8450-2 (ebook) 1. Ska (Music)--History and criticism. I. Title.
ML3535.8.A842 2013
781.646--dc23
2013016566

Printed in the United States of America

Contents

Acknowledgments

I would like to thank my family, Ron, Sid, and Frank, for putting up with my obsession. I know I am annoying and take time away from the family from time to time to research, travel, and write. I am immensely thankful for you.

To my mom, for your unconditional support and love, always. Even though you may not be interested in my subject, you always listen and encourage me: I couldn't do it without you. To my brother for taking me to my first ska show and helping me decide to take on this project. To my dad for first introducing me to the music of Jamaica.

Scott Calhoun, my editor, I am a better writer because of you. That is a massive gift. You taught me to put aside my journalism voice and embrace my own. I found a new side of me thanks to you.

Bennett Graff, thank you for finding me and trusting me with this important work. Your vision has given ska significance rather than a mere retelling of the history.

To my fellow skamrades, Brad Klein, Michael Turner, and Gus Berger—thank you for your shared passion. It's good to know I'm not crazy for my obsession, and it's good to know I can always come to you when I have a question, as you all are so much more knowledgeable than I am! Respect.

To historians Herbie Miller, Bunny Goodison, Kingsley Goodison, Clinton Hutton, and Myrna Hague-Bradshaw, thank you always for being a resource in my research. The world thanks you for your contributions to keeping ska and all Jamaican music and culture alive. Thank you for allowing me to share in your history.

Graeme Goodall, engineer extraordinaire, endless wealth of memories and stories, I can't thank you enough for your help, and most of all, your friendship and humor.

Steve Shafer of Duff Guide to Ska blog and Moon Ska Records, I owe you a beer for all the help with reconstructing East Coast ska history. It was fun reliving the '80s and '90s, and your involvement was crucial. Cheers! And Marc Wasserman of of Bigger Thomas and the Marco on the Bass blog, thank you for your wealth of information and undying love for ska.

To all of the musicians who have helped to shape my dialogue, through your conversations, through your art, thank you for gifts that cannot be quantified with words.

Series Editor Foreword

When ska comes through the speakers, it is nearly impossible to resist its rhythm, horns, and celebration of life. You can't stay still. You will dance. Ska is a music of release, composed of the tempos and sounds of release, almost to the exclusion of release's counterpoint, restraint. But in ska's persistent, infectious rhythm is the conspicuous presence of tension and restraint. Though the origins of ska lie almost a thousand years ago, amid the indigenous peoples of the Caribbean developing musical calls for both practical communication and ceremonial rites, Jamaicans—the modern world's rightful claimants to ska—struggled for freedom from European colonists from the sixteenth into the twentieth centuries. The through-line of Jamaica's history, and therefore most of ska's history, is a fight for independence, dignity, and prosperity. In ska's earliest beginnings were the notes of the essential human desire to speak and be heard and to acknowledge the more eventful occasions of life with a heightened consciousness. In many ways, the emergence of modern ska from Jamaica in the 1950s reaches right back to its origins, with its call to proclaim happiness and freedom and to celebrate life. To do these two things—sing and dance—is all the more vital for a community's survival because of Jamaicans' "do it when we can and while we can," because we can awareness of the larger cultural menaces looming over their moments of freedom.

The ska scene in Jamaica in the 1950s and 1960s had colorful moments, characters, and incidents that arose during the island's transition to independence. Ska's journey away from the island across waters near and far helps us trace moments of concentrated frustration and uncertainty among the youth culture of the contemporary Western world. It is not surprising that English youth coming of age in the 1970s embraced ska as a form of resistance against the ever-growing economic and industrial despair of British society. Neither should it surprise us that young Americans in the 1980s and 1990s turned to the jumping rhythm, joyful brass, and uplifting tempos during those two decades of increasing disparity between socioeconomic classes and of watching a government acting more like an insensitive empire overseas than an ambassador of democracy. British and American youth, both black and white, embraced ska on its own terms, but it was also absorbed into local musics developing in post-punk England and in East and West Coast pop and rock in the

United States. At times subtle, at other times pronounced, ska itself has become one of Jamaica's most effective cultural ambassadors.

Like a cultural barometer, the rise of ska indicates when and where social, political, and economic institutions disappoint their people and push them to reinvent the process for making meaning out of life. When a group embarks on this process, it becomes even more necessary to embrace expressive, liberating forms of art for help during the struggle. In its history as a music of freedom, ska has flowed freely to wherever people are celebrating the rhythms and sounds of hope.

Scott Calhoun
Tempo Series Editor

Timeline

AD 1000: Jamaica is inhabited by the Ciboney people, followed by the Arawaks, who come from Guyana or islands in the Greater Antilles and the Bahamas.

May 4, 1494: Christopher Columbus arrives on the island of Jamaica during his second voyage to the Americas.

1500: Spanish settlers colonize Jamaica and develop sugar plantations; they are followed by other European colonizers.

1517: The first slaves are brought to Jamaica.

1655: Britain conquers Spain and colonizes Jamaica. Many slaves retreat into the mountains as Maroons and establish musical forms as a means of communication and connection to Africa.

1834: Slavery is abolished in Jamaica.

Late 1700s–early 1800s: Calypso originates in Trinidad.

1860s: Revivalist cults of Pukkumina, Kumina, and Zion emerge, with music traditions blending with European religions and celebrations such as jonkunnu.

Late 1800s: Mento originates in Jamaica as calypso merges with revivalist music and jonkunnu traditions.

1880: The Alpha Boys School is founded in Kingston by Justina Ripoll, Josephine Ximenes, and Louise Dugiol.

1892: The Alpha Boys School Band is founded as a drum and fife corps.

1914–1918: World War I.

Early 1920s (possibly earlier): Jazz begins in Jamaica.

October 29, 1929: Black Tuesday marks the beginning of the Great Depression in the United States.

xi

1920s–1930s: The Harlem Renaissance produces legendary artists, including musicians Duke Ellington, Louis Armstrong, and Bessie Smith.

1939–1945: World War II.

1939: Sister Mary Ignatius Davies begins her service at Alpha Boys School and grows the boys' band program with her support.

1930s and 1940s: Burru drumming merges with Rastafarian culture at remote camps throughout the island.

1940s: American radio stations such as WNOE in New Orleans, WLAC in Nashville, and WINZ in Miami broadcast jazz.
Vere Johns begins his "Opportunity Hour" talent show, which launches dozens of careers.

June 22, 1948: The SS *Empire Windrush* sails from the Caribbean to Tilbury Dock in Essex, England, marking the beginning of mass West Indian immigration.

1950: Tom "the Great" Sebastian begins one of the first sound systems on the island, playing records from the United States, with Count Machuki toasting over the tunes.

1953: Jamaican transistor radios begin picking up a new sound from America: rhythm and blues.

1955: Rosa Parks refuses to give up her seat on a bus in Montgomery, Alabama, beginning the Montgomery bus boycott.

1950s–early 1960s: Jamaican instrumentalists gain work in orchestras and dance halls, performing for tourists and the elite.

November 18, 1956: Soviet premier Nikita Khrushchev threatens, "We will bury you!" while addressing Western ambassadors at a reception in Moscow.

Late 1950s: Duke Reid and Coxsone Dodd establish themselves in sound systems before founding the Treasure Isle and Studio One labels, respectively.

1956: Coxsone records his first song at Federal Records.

1957: Stax Records is founded by Jim Stewart and Estelle Axton in Memphis, Tennessee.

1958: Duke Reid records his first song at Federal Records.

1959: The first ska song ever recorded, "Easy Snappin'" by Theophilus Beckford, is produced by Coxsone Dodd for his Worldisc label.

1960: The Beatles form in Liverpool, England.
April 14, 1960: The Motown label is founded by Berry Gordy Jr. in Detroit, Michigan.

Early 1960s: Ska sound flourishes in studios throughout Kingston.
1960s: Musicians travel into the Wareika Hills to perform with the Burru men and Rastafarians.

1962: The Rolling Stones form in London.
August 6, 1962: Jamaica becomes

1964: The Skatalites form and back up almost all vocalists during this era as

independent from Great Britain

studio musicians and live venue performers.

Byron Lee & The Dragonaires are chosen by Edward Seaga to perform at the World's Fair in Jamaica rather than The Skatalites.

August 11–17, 1965: The Watts Riots take place in Los Angeles as a result of racial discrimination against African Americans by the LA Police Department.

January 1, 1965: Trombonist Don Drummond murders his girlfriend, Anita Mahfood, resulting in his incarceration and subsequent death in Bellevue Mental Hospital in 1969.

April 23, 1966: Haile Selassie of Ethiopia visits Jamaica. Followers by the thousands swarm the tarmac.
Summer 1966: A heat wave strikes Jamaica.

Summer 1966: Ska music's tempo slows down, horns diminish, and vocals become prominent as rocksteady takes over.

August 1969: The Woodstock music festival takes place in New York State.

1960s–1970s: Numerous Jamaican artists move to England permanently seeking better opportunities.

Late 1960s–early 1970s: Nationalist movements, including the National Front and British Movement, gain strength in England.

Late 1960s–early 1970s: Jamaican DJs and artists introduce ska and rocksteady to English youth and subcultures.

Mid-1970s: The punk movement begins in England.

1977: Jerry Dammers forms The Specials, originally called The Coventry Automatics.

1978: Los Angeles adopts a drastic desegregation plan, busing African American students miles away from their homes to historically white schools.

1979: Jerry Dammers forms the 2Tone label, which helps to launch numerous ska bands, including The Selecter, The Beat, and Madness.
1979: Fishbone forms in Los Angeles.

Late 1970s–early 1980s: Subcultures form in the United Kingdom as a result of ska music, or ska music is adopted by subcultures already formed.

Early 1980s: Rob "Bucket" Hingley moves to New York from the United Kingdom and forms The Toasters and Moon Ska Records.

Early 1981: Riots break out across England as a result of racial profiling by police during Operation Swamp.

Early 1981: The Specials record their iconic song "Ghost Town."

August 1, 1981: MTV is launched on cable television in the United States.

1981: The Untouchables form in Los Angeles.

1983: The Skatalites re-form at Sunsplash.

October 1987: Economic recession hits the United States after the largest stock market crash in history occurs on "Black Monday."

1989: The Berlin Wall comes down.

August 1990: U.S. troops enter Kuwait, beginning the First Gulf War.

September 24, 1991: Nirvana releases the album *Nevermind*, ushering in the grunge era.

1985: The Toasters release their first record, *Recriminations*, the first independently released U.S. ska record to be nationally distributed.

1986: Moon Ska Records releases *New York Beat: Hit & Run*, a compilation of East Coast bands' music.
UB40 tours the Soviet Union.

1988: Moon Ska Records releases *Ska Face*, the first compilation featuring national ska bands.

1993: The Skatalites record their first album since reuniting, *Skavoovie*.

Mid-1990s: Ska reaches the height of its popularity in the United States, and bands spring up worldwide.

Late 1997–early 1998: Ska music has saturated the U.S. market and fizzles out.

2000: Moon Ska Records closes its storefront and label.

August 22, 2002: Megalith Records is founded by Robert "Bucket" Hingley.

Fall 2012: The Skatalites continue performing, in their 48th Anniversary Tour in Europe.

Introduction

When my two boys were little, around three or four years old, like most kids their age they went through a phase of asking "why?" about almost everything. Though it may have been annoying, they were only exhibiting their childlike and very human curiosity about life. Similarly, I have entered a curious phase of my life, not only asking "why?" about aspects of life, which helps me get to the heart of things, but also asking "so what?" This question helps me to separate the wheat from the chaff, to determine what is valuable and what is worthless. As a researcher and writer, I am constantly questing for the significance of my subject. After all, if there is no big answer to my "so what?," then why bother at all?

The act of inquiry was my first route into this music called ska. I first asked "what's that?" when I heard its unique sounds. My first experience with ska was hearing a raucous, fun tune played by Madness, "House of Fun," on the British comedy show *The Young Ones*. Silly little song. I knew it wasn't like anything I had heard before, and my inquisitiveness led me to search for similar bands, then the music that was related to ska, and as the years went by and its history unfolded, I received answers. I discovered where, I determined how, and I even found out why and what and many things in between. But it wasn't until I read more obscure texts and talked with artists and historians that I was able to touch upon that elusive "so what." It was then that I heard ska in a new way.

This book is not a mere history book. It answers the "so what?" about ska or it attempts to. While looking at the reasons that ska exists—its origins in slavery and escape, its function for people oppressed by poverty and racism, and its purpose to elevate—I hope I have answered many questions that touch upon the significance of this music. It is critical not only to inquire why and how ska exists and what purpose it has served, but also to consider why ska's contribution to world music is not acknowledged. It is also necessary to look at ska as a means of expression, an instrument of communication and fellowship. And it is imperative to see how this musical genre has found its way into other musical forms to serve the purposes of connection to other cultures, expression of political passions, and release from misery.

Appreciating ska can happen without an inquiry. However, by understanding the significance of ska we can heighten our appreciation when listening to it. Through the strike of the cymbal, we can feel the searing pain of a whip. Through the haunting wail of the trombone, we can hear the barefoot boys running through puddles on their way to bed at night. Through the minor chords ascending into a major scale, we can feel the release of finding brotherhood in the hills or on the stage. We are all participants and human beings who experience ska. We, too, experience the optimism, accord, and hope. We share it with those who gave us the gift of their art, as well as with those who receive its intensity.

I hope this book will bring the reader a better appreciation for ska music. That is the only goal of all of my work. I ask "why" and "so what" and a myriad of other questions to help the reader, the listener, better savor ska, to develop a satisfaction when hearing and understanding, and to show the gravity of the people's music.

ONE

Stoking the Fire

When Jamaican musicians talk about the origins of ska music, they commonly start their stories by claiming this or that person invented the unique beat of their music. When arguing over their claim to the beat, they forget that ska's heritage goes back much further than a distinctive rhythm. Ska's roots go back hundreds of years and are intertwined with the rhythms and cultures of Jamaica's indigenous people, the Europeans who colonized their land, the slaves who were kidnapped and brought to the island, and all peoples of the Caribbean region.

ARAWAKS

It may seem strange to begin ska's history over a millennium before anyone ever heard the slide of a trombone or the "pep pep" of a toaster on the microphone, but its roots were established in the characters, traits, and interests of the native people of Jamaica and those who came afterward. Historians typically begin Jamaica's story with the arrival of Christopher Columbus during his second voyage to the Americas, on May 4, 1494. But these same accounts have Columbus and his crews being greeted by the indigenous people of the island, the Arawaks, so obviously the history, even though largely undocumented, precedes the arrival of the European conquerors. These native people are important to telling the complete story of Jamaica's history, as well as Jamaica's musical history, because from the very start, the Jamaican people have had a culture all their own, infused, through domination, with the cultures of those who came to Jamaica.

Jamaica is thought to have been inhabited by primitive people, cave dwellers called Ciboney, as far back as AD 1000. The Arawaks then came to the island, probably from Guyana or perhaps from other islands in the

Greater Antilles and the Bahamas. The Arawaks were a peaceful agricultural and fishing people, and although they were still a Stone Age people with primitive tools, they developed a musical tradition. They could also be surprisingly fierce when they needed to be, and it is from these people that Jamaicans draw their original ancestry—a tenacious yet peaceful people with a great love for music.

The Arawaks had a number of musical instruments, which they crafted and played for a variety of ceremonial purposes. They carved trumpets from hollow wood or leafstalks. They also had flutes made from wild cane and drums made from the trunk of the trumpet tree, covered by the skin of a manatee, which the Arawaks also used as a food source. The Arawaks had constructed stringed instruments and tambourines made with shells as well, reserved for the chief only to play. This musical hierarchy continued into the days of ska, as bandleaders direct their groups, and musicians considered masters of their instruments are called "chief musicians."

Constructing instruments from found materials also continued into the ska era. Not unlike the Arawaks, Johnny "Dizzy" Moore, trumpeter with the seminal ska group The Skatalites, first learned to express his love of music by constructing flutes from papaya stalks and the leaves of pumpkin plants, as well as stringed instruments from rubber bands and sardine cans. Genius musician and trombonist Don Drummond wanted to play so much as a child that he made kazoo-like instruments with a comb and paper. Headley Jones made his own cello at age fourteen and constructed a solid-body electric guitar a full year before Les Paul built his for Gibson Guitars. Lloyd Brevett, bassist for The Skatalites, learned to make his own double bass from his father, also a professional bassist who constructed his own instrument.

The Arawaks' music served a variety of purposes for their culture. Although none of their music exists today because it predates recording and was not written down, oral tradition tells us that the music served a historical purpose, relating events of the day. There were also simple songs of love, joy, and happiness. Some songs told of the Arawaks' despair over having their homes ravaged; their cassava, tobacco, and maize plants ransacked; and the killing or capture of their wives and daughters by the Carib, a vicious tribe and the enemy of the Arawaks. Nearly a millennium later, ska music continued these same musical themes, although describing different oppressors. Ska music also detailed the events of the day, such as Jamaican independence; political incidents; and activities of average people, like gossiping women in the yard, gangsters, and the man in the street. Songs of love and hope are common in ska, in both the tone as well as the lyrics of the tunes. Equally significant are ska songs about poverty, crime, and oppression.

SPANISH AND ENGLISH CONQUEST

When the Spanish settlers arrived in Xamayca, as it was originally called, they brought along their European diseases; by 1540, only four decades after the Spanish arrived on the island, the Arawaks were extinct. In the years that followed, the Spanish did little to develop the island and instead used Jamaica as a source of food for the rest of their conquering crews, who traveled around the Caribbean and Americas claiming lands as their own. They also began developing sugar plantations and employed slaves they acquired from the newly emerging Atlantic slave trade. The first slaves were brought to Jamaica in 1517.

Around 1550, settlers from France, England, Italy, Portugal, and Holland began arriving in Jamaica and throughout the Caribbean to wrest control of the area from Spain and exploit its resources. Despite resistance from the Spanish settlers and a five-year war, the British seized control of Jamaica in 1655 and established it as a colony. The British began introducing African slaves to the island en masse.

The combination of the Spanish, African, and British cultures had an enormous impact on the area's music. From this point forward, all Jamaican music became a blend of European and African sounds.

SLAVERY AND AFRICAN INFLUENCES

Most people now know that the Middle Passage was the triangular route on which kidnapped men, women, and children were brought from their homes in Africa to countries throughout the Caribbean and Americas, and also on to European countries. But many may not realize from which countries in West Africa, or more specifically, from which tribes in West Africa, the slaves came. Slaves taken to Jamaica came from tribes of the Mandingo, Coromantee, Papaw or Whidaw, Eboe, Congo, Angolo, and others. They brought no belongings, but they did carry with them their music, spirituality, and heritage, which could not be taken away, although the slave owners would try.

As sugar cultivation became a dominant industry in Jamaica, the number of slaves skyrocketed on the island as the British colonizers sought to make as much money as possible from the work of others. By 1775, there were 192,787 slaves in Jamaica, working on the plantations of the rich landowners. During these years a strong class system was established. The first class consisted of the whites who were plantation owners or professionals. The second class comprised whites who were indentured servants, sent to Jamaica from Great Britain because they were convicted of crimes in their own country. They were essentially slaves, but they could earn their freedom. The third class consisted of slaves from Africa, who suffered horrific working conditions, abuse, and poor food and had no hope of obtaining freedom.

This class system persists in Jamaica and literally divides the city of Kingston according to status, those north of Hope Road and those downtown. During the years of ska's incubation, the class system determined which musicians could perform in which clubs. The class system sent musicians like Count Ossie and his drummers into the corner to perform under no spotlight so that the upper-class clientele would not see the undesirables. This class system explains why ska music was considered a "downtown" music of the ghetto that was only palatable when performed by those with lighter skins and lighter names. Even from these early days, the class system determined how successful a musician could be decades later, despite his or her skill.

Though the slaves were forced from their homelands with no possessions, they did construct instruments in Jamaica that were similar to the ones they had had back home. They made drums of various shapes and sizes, including the gumbie, which was large, made from a hollowed tree trunk, shaped like a barrel. It was played with an open hand while another man carried it. The goombah was made from a hollowed block of wood. The goombay was also made from a hollowed tree trunk or block of wood. The gumbay was square and had a goat skin stretched taut over the top of the wood box frame. It was a hand drum with a monotonous tone. The slaves also used a Coromantee flute, made from the branches of the trumpet tree, as well as stringed instruments made from wood and gourds of native trees, such as fiddles and other bow instruments.

Slave music had a variety of purposes in Jamaica, including songs for funerals or ceremonies. The music was not overtly religious in nature, because the slaves were not converted to Christianity and came from what planters considered heathen countries. Instead, the songs were about lighthearted topics to support their spirits while working. Music was frequently improvised on the spot and reported the events of the day. The songs could also be funny, which was ironic given the desperate situation slaves were forced into, although the songs could be sung in a minor chord to reveal their underlying sadness. Perhaps these roots, the serious spine behind the light tone, are but one reason the music that followed, especially during the jazz years, the rhythm and blues (R&B) years, and the ska years, resonated so strongly with Jamaican people.

MAROONS

When the Spaniards fled the island in 1655 after the British took control, their slaves were left without masters. As a result, about fifteen hundred slaves retreated into the mountains on the east and north sides of Jamaica and established their own communities. They became known as Maroons, not because they were marooned, as one might assume, but for the Spanish word *cimarrones*, which meant wild, unruly, fugitives. These groups of fugitive slaves grew in number, and their rebellions fueled future generations in times of despair. One rebellion in Clarendon was led by a now-famous historical figure named Cudjoe, who helped to organize the Maroons. Other rebellions were led by the now-mythical figure Queen Nanny, also called Nanny of the Maroons. Rebels such as these became folk heroes and inspired the future oppressed, such as Ivanhoe "Rhyging" Martin, the subject of the film *The Harder They Come*, and the entire rudeboy culture during the ska era.

Although the Maroons were primarily Coromantee people, slaves came from other regions in Africa as well, so the Maroons were diverse and spoke a number of languages. But they needed to communicate with each other as groups settled in areas across the mountains. In addition to developing a language all their own, as well as using body language, the Maroons used music to communicate.

The Maroons used an instrument called an abeng, made from the horn of a cow, which they adapted by removing the tip to create a hole about the size of a pea. About one inch away from this opening, on the concave side of the horn, another hole was made, oval in shape, which was the mouth hole, similar to one on a flute. The Maroons had a code for communicating with each other across long distances using the abeng, which created a penetrating, blaring sound. The Maroons also used drums such as the toombah, which was similar to the Arawak tambourine and featured strings with pieces of metal across the vibrating animal skin. They also had the Coromantee flute. When not used for communication, all of the instruments were performed on during times of gathering and camaraderie. This tradition of gathering together in musical communion continued for centuries and became the cornerstone of ska music, music performed by a large group, for a large group, for the purpose of expression and common communication.

REVIVALIST CULTS

African slaves brought a number of religions with them to the Caribbean, and in the 1860s these religions merged with the Europeans' faiths, namely Christianity, especially Baptists. This movement was known as the Great Revival. From it, the cults of Pukkumina (sometimes spelled Pocomania), Kumina, and Zion emerged. These cults stemmed from the African religious practice myalism, a polytheistic religion that, when merged with monotheistic Christianity, produced a combination of the two. Followers of Pukkumina, Kumina, and Zion believed there was both a temporal world as well as a spiritual world, and that they could be possessed by spirits during ceremonies. Myal spirits were good, such as angels and saints, and obeah spirits were bad, or ghosts. Followers thought that they could catch myal by being possessed during rituals, or they could manipulate obeah against other people to bring them misfortune, thereby bringing themselves fortune. Myal spirits, which are from their god, heal, and obeah spirits are earthbound and cause injury. Zionists believed less in earthbound spirits and more in the heavenly.

Followers of a revival cult believed they were possessed by spirits during meetings, bowing the body, stamping their feet on the ground, groaning, and breathing to expel the spirits, which was called laboring. Patterns of this experience were frequently rhythmic. This display could last an hour, and sometimes the possessed fell into a trance for hours or days. Revival members referred to each other as brother or sister, and to their leaders as mother or father, a practice similar to the Rastafarian culture that played a big role in ska music.

Revivalist rituals took place during important events in life, including death. Death rituals were called a Nine Night, because revivalists believed certain rituals had to be followed out of respect for the deceased, who would otherwise return, as obeah, to torment the living. The first night featured the wake, the second or third days were the funeral. A light burned in the home for nine days when the spirit of the deceased returns. The ninth night highlighted the entire ceremony with singing and feasting until morning. A memorial service might occur on the anniversary of the departed. Nine Night is still observed by many Jamaicans today, even if they have no association with a revivalist cult. The ritual is the subject of ska vocalist Prince Buster's song, "Hard Man Fe Dead," as well as reggae/dancehall artists Steely & Clevie's "Nine Night Version," which features a rhythm used in Pukkumina.

These rhythms used in revivalist cults came directly from African ancestors. Kumina, the roots of which are in the Congo, utilized drums in its ritual, which believers sat astride while playing. Two drums were used in Kumina practice. The kbandu was typically played with a stick, had a low tone, and was used to keep a steady 4/4 rhythm. It could also be played with the hands, and the drummer, sitting astride the drum, used the heel of one foot to change the pitch of the sound. The playin kya, or playing cast, was also sometimes played with sticks, but featured a higher pitch used for the syncopation. This 4/4 rhythm was the backbone of the music that followed, and it wasn't until ska music turned it inside out that drummers experienced the rhythm in a new way.

Another instrument used in Kumina was the shaka, which was similar to the maraca or a rattle. Shakas were made from gourds or objects with shells or seeds inside. Members could participate in the music with these shakas; with a grater played with a comb; or with katta sticks or spoons used on the mission ground flagpole, empty rum bottles, or drums. Participants sang as well using a call-and-response pattern, a common form in folk music that was also mirrored in later years when Jamaican jazz music adapted this form into a theme and variation method. Like the songs of Africa meant to connect and communicate, and the work songs of the slaves with a similar function, the call-and-response format brought together the members of Kumina in a spiritual bond while communicating to the spirits. Dance was a crucial component of the Kumina ceremony. While the instrumentalists performed, the dancers participated in a frenetic display of spirit possession, improvisation, and communal expression similar to the movements utilized in the Congo. Group participation, connecting together as a group, and sharing in a common expression of creativity, in both collective performance and dance, set the foundation for the musical forms that followed.

CARNIVAL AND JONKUNNU

Much of the showmanship and competition found in the music industry in Jamaica today and throughout the last century can be traced back to the pomp and swagger of the Caribbean festivals, at which music and performance combined in a flamboyant display of prowess. These festivals—carnival in Trinidad and jonkunnu in Jamaica—were celebrations that took place during the height of the Great Revival and continue today. Jonkunnu has its origins in the carnival celebration in Trinidad, which in turn had its origins in the masquerade celebrated by Europeans. Carnival began at Christmastime and lasted sometimes until Ash Wednesday. Celebrations included feasting and processions through the streets, the biggest of which took place on Shrove Tuesday, or the Tuesday before Ash Wednesday.

These processions were called canboulay, a derivation of the French words *cannes brulees*, which translate as burning canes. The story behind the canboulay is that while slaves were carrying burning canes as torches to light the way during the night, a plantation owner's crops caught fire. Slaves from nearby plantations were summoned to help extinguish the fire. Forced into the field by a driver with a whip, the slaves carried flaming torches to light the way. Canboulay processions drew elements from these events. Participants with whips emulated the slave master, and masked characters represented people and animals, in an entertaining lampoon of life. The meaning behind these processions was serious, but the tone was lighthearted and enjoyable.

One of the main displays in canboulay during carnival was kalinda. Kalindas were stick fights, similar to the art of dula meketa in Ethiopia or mousondi in the Congo, and were tests of strength and skill. During carnival, a group or band of some two dozen men was led by a "big pappy," who directed his crew through the streets until they encountered a rival group. In a spirit of camaraderie and competition, members of each group boasted about their prowess and issued challenges, frequently set to music, which was called kalinda, because the warlike song and the stick fight itself were part of the festival procession. Fighters chose their sticks carefully, visiting a region in Trinidad called Gasparillo to select a stick made of Baton Gasparee wood. They then prepared their sticks by singeing them over a fire until the bark came off, then rubbing coconut oil into the wood. When horns or empty bottles were sounded, the bands assembled, accompanied by instrumentalists, singers, and dancers, who performed a dance called a belair, or bele. The display involved the participation of all, and the boasting was competitive in a respectful, boisterous, convivial manner. This spirit of competitive cama-raderie continued in the days of sound system clashes in the 1950s and 1960s, as producers attempted to one-up each other to appeal to the crowds. And ska recording artists, following the lead of the big pappies, also threw down challenges to each other, boasting about their talent.

Because of the perceived threat of violence and revolt, canboulay and kalindas were banned by the government and police after riots in 1881. The masks used by characters in the procession were also banned in festivals in 1840 by the British governor. Drums and fiddles, associated with Africa, were considered heathen and therefore instruments of the devil; they were also loud and disturbing late at night. Open letters in local newspapers called the revelers "savages" and spoke of celebrations as "orgies" full of "crime" and "barbarism." The people resisted, but they were quashed by military troops, forced to either conform to the estab-lishment or adapt the festival so as to elude the authorities.

In Jamaica, this festival was called jonkunnu, named after John Con-ny, a powerful leader of the Guinea people in the early 1700s. The British spelled his name John Canoe, hence the name jonkunnu. The white plant-ers allowed their slaves to celebrate this secular festival, which took place during the Christmas season. Elaborate street parades began on the is-land as early as 1774. Like carnival, jonkunnu involved masked charac-ters. Performance and music always went hand in hand. The leader of the festival wore cow horns and a cow tail and sometimes carried swords or wore a mask with tusks. This character was John Canoe. Other characters included those mocking the military, aristocrats, police, sailors, the devil, Horsehead, Jack-in-the-Green, Pitchy-Patchy, Belly Woman, Warrior, Red Indian or Wild Indian, Koo-Koo or Actor Boy, King and Queen, and Red-Set and Blue-Set Girls. These characters did not remove their masks in public, nor did they speak or sing.

Those who provided the vocal and instrumental accompaniment for the procession included a band of drummers, bamboo fife, banjo, and metal grater performers. Tambour-bamboo bands also provided percus-sion by banging together lengths of bamboo or using a piece to knock on the ground. Because they were hollow, the bamboo lengths produced varying tones. Soon, musicians sought other items for percussion as well, especially because the stick bands were prohibited by the British government. Participants used household items such as spoons, bottles, and metal pans. In Trinidad, this progression soon led to the use of oil drums, which were crafted to produce different notes and tones, and the steel bands were born. But everyone was a participant; jonkunnu was not a spectator event. Everyone performed, everyone played, everyone danced, and this custom was always a part of the people's music.

BURRU

The Burru, a group of men who influenced ska musicians through their association with Rastafarianism, emerged during the slavery era on the island. Bands of Burru, African drummers, were permitted by slave owners to play drums and sing for the workers in the Jamaican fields to raise the slaves' spirits—not for emotional reasons, but to improve productivity. After slavery was abolished, the Burru could not find work, so they congregated in the impoverished areas of Kingston in the early 1900s. Their drumming style, like the African vocal styles, followed a call-and-response format, with a drum leading the rhythm, followed by "licks" from the answering drums.

Each Christmas season, the Burru men gathered to compose their own music, with words about local events or about people in the community who had committed acts of wrongdoing. They worked on these songs starting in September, and then on the holiday they traveled throughout the community, in a procession not unlike jonkunnu, going from home to home, playing their bamboo scrapers, shakas, and rhumba boxes for percussion and singing their songs, which were intended to purge the evil of the previous year before the new one began. Although the music was composed during the months before the event, the musicians also improvised on the spot, a practice that was continued in the traditions of subsequent musical forms, such as jazz, ska, and reggae. Because the Burru were mischievous in their songs and lived in the slum areas of the city, they were mistakenly considered by many to be criminals or undesirables. In the 1930s and 1940s, the Burru went to live with the Rastafarians at camps throughout the mountains, especially in Kingston, and the music of the Burru combined with the spirituality of the Rastafarians, as they found solace together from society's rejection. These camps became a refuge for musicians during the ska era as well, because they were a place for uninhibited musical communion, for performance without restriction or limitations, and for retreat from the hardships of an oppressive life.

CALYPSO

One might think that calypso music evolved from the steel bands, because they have a similar tone and lyrics that can be political and social, and one might also think calypso evolved from carnival; there is certainly a direct link to both. But calypso also has a connection to the gayap, the work song sung by slaves in the fields. When slaves, or after slavery, African contract workers were gathered together to clear a field, they frequently sang gayapes, led in a call-and-response format. Bands of workers in the field, gathered into clusters of one or two dozen, sang the gayapes to each other in the same spirit of the stick bands, issuing challenges and boasts and belittling the other groups for their work in a spirit of competition, until the work was complete and ended in a mass feast and celebration. The boasting tradition continued in in sound system clashes, and musical competition found its roots.

Calypso is the culmination of all these folk forms that had come to the Caribbean from Africa and Europe. Trinidadian playwright and historian Errol Hill writes that calypso, also called kaiso, has "the major types of traditional songs functionally associated with the people of Trinidad and Tobago. Examples of these are the digging songs chanted by people at work; belair and calinda songs when they play; shango and shouter Baptist revival songs when they worship; and insurrectionary songs such as were sung by slaves in revolt" (Hill, 1971, p. 23). Calypso melodies were influenced by the Spanish, Venezuelans, French, Irish, and English. Calypso was a mélange of these forms, and because culture in the Caribbean was fluid, this musical form quickly came to Jamaica as musicians and vocalists traveled from hotel to hotel, performing for tourists and locals alike.

Originally performed during carnival in Trinidad between stick-fighting bouts as an entertainment interlude, calypso may date as far back as 1784, to a professional singer known as Gros Jean. Calypsos were sung in an African tongue, patois, or French Creole; in the late 1800s, Richard the Lion Heart, Norman LeBlanc, introduced the first English calypsos. To prepare for carnival, calypso artists assembled in a tent days before the event to write and practice, but the form was also extemporaneous, with musicians improvising on the spot to compete against one another with fresh material. Soon audiences were not only attending carnival to participate in the festivities, including hearing the calypsos, but were also attending the tent practices, which then became an event all their own.

To complement the boastful challenges that constituted the content of the calypsos, singers, called chantrels, took stage names that reflected their prowess, a convention that many ska artists and producers later adopted. Calypso monikers like King Pharaoh, Mighty Duke, Lord Superior, Black Prince, Lord Executor, Mighty Sparrow, and Lord Inventor are indicative of this trend. The songs were witty and funny; could be narrative or expository of the singers' abilities and skill; ridiculed and besmirched rivals, frequently the slave master and his exploitation; and were displays of verbal bravado. Musically, calypso incorporated the same instruments of carnival: drums, graters, shakers, stick percussion, and stringed instruments. Women usually provided backup to the chantrels. Bands dressed in colorful, fancy costumes of velvet, fine silk, or other fabrics trimmed with ribbons, braids, plumes, and gilt decorations to set themselves apart from other bands and make an impression on the judges of the competition. Once again, music and performance were one and the same. Everyone participated, both the musicians and the audience, in a shared experience of musical communion.

There were a number of themes in calypso music, aside from the songs of protest. According to Agatha Lowe, some calypsos also addressed health topics: "Health themes in calypso have been evident since the late forties and fifties, and have reflected some of the health problems prevalent at the time. Thus, during an outbreak of meningitis, people were advised to keep up their health and 'Drink cold eddo soup / A piece of boiled shark / On mornings two fried eggs / And break meningitis legs'" (1995, p. 61). Another theme was family planning: "Prior to the 1960s the mother in calypso tended to be revered, whereas other women were presented as sex objects, untrustworthy, and as trying to trick men into marriage" (1995, p. 61). Much later, subjects like AIDS and drug abuse figured in calypso's themes.

MENTO

In Jamaica during the late 1800s, elements of calypso, along with the revivalist music and carnival music, merged with African roots to produce a new genre, mento. Because of the common timeline of calypso and mento and the similarity in their sound, many people either confuse the two or mention both in the same breath, but despite their kinship, mento is clearly different from calypso in many ways. Some people contend that this kinship may be tenuous and more a feature of marketing than anything else. The relationship, especially because of geography, may be closer between mento and the son music of Cuba, which is some one thousand miles closer to Jamaica than Trinidad and lent itself to exchange through labor migration. *Son*, the Spanish word for sound, had its origins in the sixteenth century, and like the forms previously discussed, served the purpose of relaying details of recent events and had an African call-and-response format, a form reflected in the theme and variation of jazz and ska in later years.

Emerging in Jamaica in the late 1800s, mento used instruments such as drums, tambourines, graters played with the handle of a spoon, fifes, fiddles, and even the concertina, the small, bellowed instrument related to the accordion. Later, mento incorporated one or two banjos played like guitars rather than in a picking style; a rhumba box, which is a large mbira or kalimba structured into a box that is sat on when played; and guitars. The fife and later a harmonica, woodwind, or keyboard performed the melody. The stringed instruments and rhumba box played the harmony. Rhythm came from the drums and other percussive instruments, such as the graters, maracas, and even body sounds, much like ska music, in which rhythm is central. But the voice is the most important component of mento music, an aspect that makes it very different from ska.

Mento has assimilated with an array of other musical dance forms over the years, such as quadrilles, reels, jigs, polkas, and waltzes. It also resets or "covers" other songs into a unique rhythm that distinguishes it from other forms, a practice that continued when Jamaicans covered American R&B music in the 1940s and 1950s, as well as in the ska era, when Jamaicans covered songs by all sorts of musicians, from Johnny Cash to Mongo Santamaria. Original mento lyrics may comment on social events of the day, often with a witty tone, or use sexual innuendo, such as "Big Bamboo," by Duke of Iron; "Juicy Oyster," by Everard Williams and Alerth Bedasse; "Watermelon Man," by Count Premier; "Cutting Wood," sung by Louise Lamb, with lyrics by Everard Williams; "Rough Rider," by Chin's Calypso Sextet; and "Slide Mongoose," by Count Lasher. Lyrics were always upbeat, happy, and funny, even if they were just a description of some Jamaican recipe or food or an account of daily life. Singers were frequently male, but some women made their mark as well, like Louise Lamb, the great Louise Bennett, and Girl Wonder, who is said to be Rita Marley.

The mento form is also distinguished by its rhythm and stylistic pattern. Mentos always have a quadruple meter, which means there are four beats per measure, just like ska. They characteristically put a rhythmic accent on the second and fourth beats of the measure, but unlike calypso, the other instruments provide syncopation to that rhythm. Calypso has a regular quarter note accent. Mento musicians, just like the musicians in the jazz and ska eras, work together as a tight team, playing off one another's rhythm. Among early mento musicians were Slim and Sam, Lord Fly, Sugar Belly and Count Lasher, and Lord Flea.

Dance is a crucial component of mento music, and the style of dance is unique to this genre. In his 1910 book *In Jamaica and Cuba*, Herbert DeLisser describes this dance as consisting

> of slow movements of the body . . . the dancer never allows the upper part of her body to move as she writhes and shuffles over the ground. You dance with your partner alone. If you are refined, your motions may be a trifle suggestive—hardly even that. If you are not refined, they may be coarsely, brutally, blatantly vulgar. Known as the mento, the banboula, the chia, you will find this dance wherever the African was taken as a slave, and you may see it danced in many a West Indian drawing-room without the slightest suspicion that what you are hearing, or even dancing, is a sublimated West African phallic dance. (DeLisser, 1910, p. 109)

In a similar vein, special dances, like the mashed potato, twist, hully gully, stroll, and others, became a colossal craze in the United States in the 1960s, spawning "the ska" or the skank as a way to market Jamaican music to the masses.

CULTURAL IMPACT OF FOLK MUSIC IN JAMAICA

The types of folk and indigenous music in Jamaica are extensive, and variations on the forms discussed here can be found throughout the island's villages and communities, which adapted the music to suit their own needs and reflect their own heritages. Other forms of music typically use drums to accompany dances such as ettu, tambu, quadrille, maypole, brukins, and dinky mini. During the island's early days, the period of slavery, and among the cultures and groups after emancipation, music played an essential role in the lives of individuals. Not only did it bring pleasure to those enduring insufferable conditions, but it brought everyone a sense of hope, a tradition that was continued in later years, especially during the era of ska music. Music acted as a binding force for the slaves, the lower classes, the sufferers. It allowed people to transcend their poverty and powerlessness. Music brought importance and bound individuals together into communities and families, erasing loneliness, desperation, and depression. Folk music is both the music and the folk, the people and the music. They are intertwined and connect the community. No longer is the individual a poverty-stricken peasant, but rather a part of the larger world, with the power of the spirits, the power of the performance, the power to transcend one's situation and have a voice.

The processional aspect of this music also served the purpose of bringing people together to bond, uplift, and empower the individual. The West African Yoruba word for parade, *pagbo*, means to join together in a circle. This communal joining together is an essential function of the processional folk music. Unlike other forms of music, the folk music of Jamaica and the Caribbean and what followed is not performed alone or for an audience. It is performed for participation. It is an act. There is no separation between the music and the musician and the dancer. There is no passive listener.

There is also a mystical, spiritual component to Jamaican folk music. Music and performance, through the conduit of the masked character or a group leader or one who called the song to which the others responded, served to control the destiny of the village or the group members. They did have influence and a role in the events of their lives, aided by myal or obeah. Slavery may have stripped Jamaicans of control over life on earth, but in the spiritual world, the world that had dominion over the events of the earth, Jamaicans had ties, had access to the strings to pull to make the spirits move in the ways they needed to survive. Music brought back their ancestral power, their homeland, their culture, to the people, and it was a way to have hope and some power over the elements of living that people had no control over.

TWO

Music Is My Occupation

Just as West African traditions came to the Caribbean and mingled with indigenous and European forms to create a mélange of musical styles, so did these West African roots take hold in America through the slave trade. In New Orleans, Harlem, Chicago and cities all over the United States, the sounds of black and white folk music blended with European structures and African rhythms to produce big band, jazz, and R&B. Jamaicans caught wind of these sounds through the transmission of radio waves from the United States to the island and through the sale of vinyl to connoisseurs of the sound and enterprising businessmen looking to make a shilling or two, or three.

JAZZ IN JAMAICA

Jazz came to Jamaica in the early 1920s, perhaps even earlier, as a result of the tourist industry, which had become a dominant part of the island's economy. Historian and vocalist Myrna Hague-Bradshaw in her lectures for the Jamaica Music Museum has uncovered research suggesting that jazz may in fact have originated in Jamaica rather than New Orleans. Nevertheless, jazz in America flourished in the 1930s with the swing and bebop genius of Charlie Parker, Benny Goodman, Dizzy Gillespie, and dozens more. Wealthy Americans traveled to Jamaica as its tourist boards marketed the "cosmopolitan" island for the "jet set." The rich came to stay at palatial hotels and hear in-vogue tunes played by top-notch musicians. Hotels like the Myrtle Bank Hotel in Kingston, Tower Isle Hotel in Ocho Rios, and others on the north shore booked their own orchestras to perform the big band and jazz standards. Clubs in Kingston and around the island hosted performances for those who could afford the price of admission.

On specific nights, especially on holidays, Kingston theaters like the Ward Theatre, Carib Theatre, Palace Theatre, Little Theatre, Regal Theatre, Tropical Theatre, Queens Theatre, and Majestic Theatre featured a lineup of Jamaican jazz musicians or a headlining act from America, such as Sarah Vaughn or Dave Brubeck. Other dance halls, like the Jubilee Tile Gardens on Upper King Street, the Forresters Hall on North Street, and Bartleys Silver City on East Queen Street, had road bands that would rotate in and out on a given night. But the clubs frequented by tourists and paying locals, such as the Colony Club, Bournemouth Beach Club, Glass Bucket Club, and Silver Slipper, had their own resident orchestras to attract tourists every night. Popular orchestra leaders included Eric Deans, Sonny Bradshaw, Baba Motta, Lester Hall, Roy Coburn, Vivian Hall, Tony Brown, and Kenny Williams. Orchestra leaders obtained jazz music scores from England and the United States and arranged their musicians on stage behind bandstands that displayed the name of the orchestra and its leader.

Jamaicans also had another source to feed their love of jazz, one that was less about commercial gain and more about personal enjoyment. In 1941, the U.S. Air Force opened Vernam Field, thirty miles southwest of Kingston in the parish of Clarendon. The base served the purpose of patrolling for enemy submarines in the Caribbean during World War II, because German U-boats were a growing threat. In the same year, the U.S. Navy opened an air station at Portland Bight, an area in southern St. Catherine, just to the east of Kingston Harbor. Both bases were leased to the U.S. military by the British Crown. Soldiers staying at the base, or coming in and going out of the base, brought a steady supply of American music with them, especially to play at the USO club, which was located on Old Hope Road. Jamaicans, who have always had a fascination with American culture, bought records from the men and heard the soldiers playing the music on base and in the USO club. These Jamaicans were either wealthy or crafty, owning their own turntables or making their own. Some sold the records to those who could play them.

Regular folk who were lucky enough to find someone who owned a transistor radio, frequently the landlord of a tenement yard, could listen to the American radio stations broadcasting jazz, such as WNOE in New Orleans, WLAC in Nashville, and WINZ in Miami. The island's only radio station in the early days, ZQI (which became RJR in 1950), did not play jazz during the one-hour-a-week initial broadcasts, which eventually grew to a whopping four hours a day. This station mostly played news, war updates, BBC relay broadcasts, or local classical music.

ALPHA BOYS SCHOOL

With so much love for jazz, where did club and theater owners find their pool of talent? They turned to one of Jamaica's leading schools for training musicians, Alpha Boys School, an incubator for the most talented musicians on the island. Dozens of performers who were trained in the Alpha Boys School Band went on to appear on stages all over the world. Alpha Boys School was founded by Justina Ripoll, better known as Jessie Ripoll, in 1880, when she and her two devout Catholic friends, Josephine Ximenes and Louise Dugiol, combined their money and bought land to establish an orphanage. They chose forty-three acres in south-central Kingston and built an orphanage for girls, a single, small cottage. When the doors officially opened, one young girl was given a home and the love and care of three mothers. Their devotion to the children of Kingston grew as child after child came to call the school home. Alpha Cottage School, as it was then named, first welcomed boys in 1883.

Unable to support the orphanage on their own, the three founders joined with a group of nuns from the Roman Catholic Sisters of Mercy in London, who traveled to Kingston to establish a mission in 1890. In addition to expanding their orphanage, the three founders also became nuns in the order. Jessie Ripoll became known as Sister Mary Peter Claver, Josephine Ximenes as Sister Mary Joseph, and Louise Dugiol as Sister Margaret Mary.

On August 20, 1890, the Jamaican government allowed the Sisters of Mercy to register Alpha as an industrial school and began funding the institution, which had twelve boys at the time. Over the years, nuns from many countries, such as England, Malta, the United States, Canada, and Panama, came to serve at Alpha and help guide the students, as many as seven hundred at times. These sisters assisted in teaching classes in addition to instructing the students, who came to Alpha from a variety of unfortunate situations, in trades they could use to gain employment after they left school, such as gardening, printmaking, book binding, pottery, plumbing, shoemaking, tailoring, woodworking, and music.

Most boys who attended Alpha from the 1940s through the 1990s remember their surrogate mother, who truly made Alpha Boys School a home. Sister Mary Ignatius Davies was crucial in mentoring, educating, and raising the boys at Alpha, and she single-handedly shaped the course of the music there with her passion and devotion to the boys. One could easily argue that without Sister Ignatius, ska and the resulting genres rocksteady, reggae, dancehall, and dub would have looked so different as to be unrecognizable.

Sister Mary Ignatius Davies, affectionately called Sister Iggy, was born in Jamaica in 1921 in Innswood, St. Catherine. She moved to Kingston as a child, where she attended Mico Elementary School and then became a student at the Alpha Academy, the girls' section of the institution. Sister

Ignatius became a member of the Sisters of Mercy, or a nun, shortly after her graduation from school, because she felt a calling to that way of life, and she started serving at the Alpha Boys School in 1939.

Sister Ignatius's tutelage was vital to the students whom many called "wayward boys." She trained them by building their characters; playing games with them in the yard; putting on gloves and boxing with them; and playing music on her own deejay equipment, which she used to instruct and entertain. Her collection of hundreds of records encompassed a variety of musical genres, including classical, jazz, Latin, and even spoken word from Malcolm X. She sent students to record stores with a list of her selections and a handful of money so she could keep up on the latest musical trends and share them with her boys. She also played the saxophone and would periodically perform with the Alpha Boys Band.

Once described by Pierre Perrone, a reporter at *The Independent*, as "bird-like" because of her diminutive stature, Sister Ignatius had a great love for music. It was because of her passion for all kinds of music that the band program prospered. This program at Alpha Boys School was established in 1892 as a drum and fife corps, then was bolstered up in 1908 when a Roman Catholic bishop in Jamaica donated a number of brass instruments to the school. The same year, Walter S. Harrison became a drill sergeant at the school, appointed by the Jamaica Defense Force. He served as the inaugural bandmaster for one year, then continued on as drill sergeant through the mid-1960s. As a result, there was a strong connection between Alpha and the military. After graduation from Alpha, boys frequently took positions in the West Indian Regiment, which became the Jamaica Military Band after independence. Music taught during the band's early years was solely classical. But under the leadership of Sister Ignatius, the band program expanded, because she saw opportunities in music for her boys after they left Alpha. The band program also grew during Sister Ignatius's years because music, like her boys and her spirituality, was her love.

Band boys trained at Alpha either joined the military bands, which provided a reasonable living, or entered the jazz club circuit. Orchestra leaders like Eric Deans scouted Alpha Boys School when they had a seat to fill, sometimes even taking boys out of school early, a move supported by Sister Ignatius. After all, the goal for the trades at Alpha was to obtain skills for employment. Master trombonist Don Drummond left Alpha this way in 1950, six weeks before graduation, as did Eddie "Tan Tan" Thornton and Wilton Gaynair, among others. Other musicians, like saxophonist Bertie King, left Alpha in the 1930s. After leading his own orchestra in Kingston, King went to England in 1936 to pursue more opportunity, although he returned to Jamaica over the course of his career. Trumpeter Dizzy Reece graduated from Alpha and went to England in 1948, where he had a fruitful career performing throughout Europe. Alto saxo-

phonist Joe Harriott also left for England, in 1951, years after his graduation from Alpha. Harriott found success as a bebop and free-form jazz
musician. The epitaph on his grave states, "Parker? There's them over
here can play a few aces too."

Promised a life of lucrative gigs, traveling at times to clubs all over the
Caribbean, for the Alpha Boys, learning to play an instrument was a skill
not unlike learning to weld, print, or turn a table leg on a lathe. Music
was an occupation. "Most of the musicians who came out of Alpha were
largely jazz musicians," writes Dermot Hussey, Jamaican music historian
(Porter, 2004). They found work in clubs performing for orchestra leaders
George Moxey, Count Buckram, Sonny Bradshaw, Carlisle Henriques,
Vivian Hall, Jack Brown, Roy Coburn, Eric Deans, John Brown, Milton
McPherson, Redver Cooke, Val Bennett, and Roy White, to name a few.
Author David Katz states, "Pretty much anyone in Jamaican music, at
some time or another, played in a hotel band, because that's where the
money was" (Porter, 2004).

Throughout the 1930s and 1940s, and even into the 1950s, jazz music
was the standard at all the posh clubs around Kingston and Jamaica. But
traveling with a ten- or fifteen-piece jazz outfit and all of the equipment
to hotels for guest appearances was tough, especially on the treacherous,
narrow, rural roads of the island, as well as expensive. At the same time,
the sound was changing in the tenement and government yards, streets,
and stores, where a different music was brewing—one that was also
brought to Jamaica from the United States, but not on boats or vinyl. This
new popular sound was more in tune with the ear of the Kingston oppressed, with its lyrics about tough times and survival.

AMERICAN RHYTHM AND BLUES

The music on the tenement yard landlords' transistor radios began to
change around 1953 or 1954 as American stations broadcast less jazz and
more of a new sound called rhythm and blues (R&B). More and more
people had access to these radios, which began to replace the old-fash-
ioned vacuum-tube radios. As a result, R&B proliferated on the island.
Tenants gathered to hear the latest tunes by American artists like Jimmy
Reed, Bill Doggett, Lloyd Price, Earl Hines, Nat King Cole, Billy Eckstine,
Jesse Belvin, and the Moonglows, who were massively popular in the
Kingston streets. The songs that came crackling through the radio, into
the squalor of the zinc-walled yards, into homes where the domestics
worked peeling bammies and washing floors, were doo-wop, toe-tapping
tunes with a blues spine and a free-spirited feel.

In the mid- to late 1950s, American R&B acts began to tour Jamaica as
well, to entertain the tourists and the wealthy elite. Bill Haley and the
Comets, Rosco Gordon, The Platters, and Louis Armstrong all came to

Jamaica to perform in 1957. That same year, a large bill of musicians performed at the Carib Theatre, including the Teenchords, Clarence "Frogman" Henry, and Bull Moose Jackson and the Buffalo Bearcats. The R&B show, called "Rock-a-Rama," lasted for two days, and its success ushered in even more American acts the following year, such as Woody Herman and Carmen Cavallaro.

Jamaicans had a natural penchant for American R&B because of its African roots. American R&B featured prominent drums with simple syncopation, horns used to add ornamentation to the harmony, and lyrics that reflected the pain and struggle of everyday life. This was the music that ska artists drew on when they played in big bands with big horn sections, taking inspiration from jazz as well. Lester Sterling, saxophonist with the seminal ska band The Skatalites, recalls, "So we used to play at the local clubs. We were playing the popular music. Fats Domino type of music, bluesy like, you know? We play together. This group of guys used to meet and talk about jazz. We weren't the guys that talk about calypso. We talk about jazz. And we talk about jazz bands like Charlie Parker, Sonny Rollins, Clifford Brown, Dizzy Gillespie. We used to talk about good musicians in general mostly" (1997 interview). Lloyd Brevett, double bassist with The Skatalites, says, "When we started, we never started in ska. We started in jazz. We were in separate bands at that point in Jamaica. Big band we started. I was 14 when I started to play in big band. It was jazz and ballads. We started to play rhythm and blues, but jazz was still with it" (1997 interview).

But after World War II, the island's economy took a downward turn and tourism declined. The wealthy no longer flocked to the clubs as they had done in the 1930s and early 1940s. Club owners had to find some way to bring in revenue. Enterprising young men who had family businesses to support launched a lucrative industry that either helped to make musicians stars or exploited their talents.

"VERE JOHNS OPPORTUNITY HOUR"

To help balance their books on off nights, theaters began to tap into the pool of local talent to fill the stage and seats. Vere Johns, a theater manager, is credited with launching this trend. After working for many years in the newspaper industry, Johns turned to offering crowds a variety show on nights when the spaghetti Westerns and musicals weren't flickering on screens throughout the island. The idea for a variety show came from Vere Johns's second wife, Lillian Margaret May Johns, who thought that entertainment competitions could bring in extra money. The competitions took place at the Palace Theatre. The show was very successful, and it was replicated at the other theaters Johns managed, such as the Majestic, Ward, Carib, Queens, Gaiety, and Ambassador. Many artists, including dancers, instrumentalists, vocalists, comedians, and even performers on bicycles, got their start through the "Vere Johns Opportunity Hour." Ten acts appeared on each bill and admission was less than a shilling. Vere Johns auditioned performers each Tuesday and Thursday at 3:00 pm. Winners were selected based solely on audience approval; whoever received the loudest applause at the end of the night won the show. Needless to say, this form of selection allowed plenty of opportunity for corruption, such as packing the house with one's own friends or supporters or paying off people to clap for a chosen artist. After the artists performed, Vere Johns stepped onto the stage and held the cash prize of £2 over each person's head until the audience responded with the appropriate level of applause. Sometimes after a performer won, audience members approached the winner in a threatening manner to demand part of the spoils. Performers who won or came in second returned the next week to perform again, so the corruption continued. As on the modern TV shows *American Idol* or *X Factor*, winning the popular talent contests assured performers success on the musical circuit. The experience was more important for the exposure than for the money. Those who got their start through the "Vere Johns Opportunity Hour" include Desmond Dekker, Alton Ellis, John Holt, Laurel Aitken, Bob Andy, Derrick Morgan, The Wailers, and Anita Mahfood.

Artists like Laurel Aitken performed the latest R&B styles at these shows to win over the crowds. Aitken, who won his first competition for Vere Johns at the age of fifteen in 1942, recalled the early days of his career: "In the '50s and '60s, we used to dance to American music, New Orleans music, rhythm and blues. Roscoe Gordon, Smiley Lewis, Big Joe Turner, and Lou Jordan, boogie-woogie, rhythm and blues" (1997 interview).

SOUND SYSTEMS

For a number of years, radio was not readily available on the island or accessible to most Jamaicans, who could not afford a set of their own. Many Jamaicans could not afford to buy tickets to see the variety shows or go to the hotel clubs to see the latest singers or orchestras. Still, they wanted to hear the latest R&B sounds from the States. To address this desire and also sell liquor, sound systems were born among a variety of groups of downtown dwellers.

Sound systems were already in full swing during the jazz era as clubs hired deejays to play during the twenty- to thirty-minute intermissions between band sets. But the sound systems in the 1950s and 1960s were much larger, because they had to project to not just a room full of people, but an entire outdoor area and beyond. Jamaican sound system operators and their selectors, or deejays, played their records on hi-fis or more powerful systems, speakers built into wood cabinets known as "houses of joy." The bigger they were, the more people they could attract with their massive sound. Deejays played the hottest American R&B, which they frequently obtained through their off-season employment as migrant workers in the southern United States when it allowed more temporary farmworkers into the country after World War II.

One of the first sound system operators was Tom the Great Sebastian, or Tom Wong, who played his records at Slipe Road at the Torrington Bridge. Other operators were Nick the Champ, Count Smith the Blues Blaster, Bells, King Edwards, Skyrocket, V-Rocket, Admiral Comic, Prince Buster, and Lord Koo's the Universe. But the two most popular sound system operators were Clement Seymour Dodd, better known as Sir Coxsone, nicknamed after a famous British cricket player, or Downbeat, after the name of his sound system; and Arthur Reid, better known as Duke Reid or The Trojan, after the make of the imported kit van he used to shuttle his equipment. Their ranking monikers of nobility, like those used by others in the business, reflected the titles adopted by calypso artists and reclaimed the colonial throne as their own.

Sound system operators like Coxsone and Duke Reid had one goal in mind from the start all the way to the end of their careers: to make money. These two fiercest competitors, who literally mashed it up over the rights to the crown, both had an interest in drawing more business to their families' liquor stores. Get people to come listen to music and dance, and you get them to drink. Recording engineer Graeme Goodall says, "People don't realize that the sound systems were the ones who drove the whole record business and what drove the sound systems and the record business was literally every one of them were liquor distributors. If they could get the crowd in there they'd sell more liquor and that's where they made their money" (July 13, 2011). Making sure the music could be heard for miles around ensured that people would flock to the yard, so speakers were strategically placed to project to the biggest space possible.

The deejays who worked for the soundmen, such as Blackie, who worked for Coxsone, were showmen, playing the crowd and dancing the coolest moves, such as shuffling their feet, smooth like an old school stepper, a different dance for each song. Other deejays, like Dodd's Count Machuki, "toasted" over the R&B tunes, skatting in a sort of percussive flourish of witticism, nonsense rhymes, gibberish, and one-upmanship reminiscent of the carnival stick fights. Count Machuki, born Winston Cooper, is widely considered the first toaster, with his washboard-like tisking or peps that punctuated the rhythm, along with comments such as, "dig it, man, dig it!" and "come on, come on" or "have some mercy on me baby," to encourage the crowd to dance, and other more creative remarks, such as, "You comin' from town, your face turn to dis sound, on your way up, or on your way down, I want you to stop at dis station for identification, I'm going to turn you over to your sound dimension, your music producer, everybody on the ball!" Count Machuki, who was skilled at attracting and keeping a crowd, first began toasting for Tom the Great Sebastian and then went to work for Coxsone.

Machuki says he was so popular with the crowds that they were disappointed by the recorded version of the live performance, solidifying the idea that ska is very much a live experience. "There would be times when the records playing would, in my estimation, sound weak, so I'd put in some peps: chick-a-took, chick-a-took, chick-a-took. That created a sensation! So there were times when people went to the record shop and bought those records, took them home, and then brought them back, and say, 'I want to hear the sound I hear at the dancehall last night!' They didn't realize that was Machuki's injection in the dancehall!" (Barrow and Dalton 1997, p. 19).

"Toasting was developed by the sound-system operators," writes Mohair Slim. "To emphasi[ze] the music's rhythm, the DJs chanted staccato noises over the top of the instrumental tracks that were the staple of the early dancehall. A common technique was the rapid-fire repetition of words, like 'ska-ska-ska' or 'get-up-get-up-get-up' also employed were locomotive-noises ('ch-ch, ch-ch, ch-ch'), hiccups ('he-da, he-da, he-da') and grunts. Prince Buster, Coxsone Dodd, and Byron Lee all utilised toasting to accentuate the fervour of their records" (n.d.).

Legendary historian and artist Clinton Hutton says the toasting had a deeper impact on the power of the sound system:

> The mike gave the voice reach and agency. The deejay could talk to the fans in the dancehall as well as to the persons outside of the dancehall. He could advertise the next dance and venue that the sound system would be playing at. He could praise the sound system owner/operator and help to brand his name and enterprise in the minds of the people. The disc jockey could dedicate a song or songs to a specific person or group of persons. He could announce the names of persons going off to England or coming from prison. Yes, he could really "wake the town and tell the people," to use a line from Daddy U-Roy. He could cover the weaknesses in a selection with live jive, with toasting, with scatting, with bawl out. (2007, p. 24).

Although there were sound system operators on many streets in Kingston and throughout the island, most consider the big three to be Duke Reid, Coxsone Dodd, and Vincent "King" Edwards. Duke Reid, born in 1915, was older than Coxsone; Reid and Coxsone's parents were good friends. Reid was a tough man, a former Kingston police officer for ten years during a time of terrible police corruption. Reid and his wife, Lucille, owned a liquor store called Treasure Isle Liquors, which they built after Lucille won the Jamaican lottery. In an effort to sell more liquor, Reid began hosting dances at the corner of Beeston Street and Pink Lane and later moved to Bond Street and Charles Street, as well as at other venues like the Success Club and Forresters Hall. Reid was flashy and attracted attention everywhere he went. He frequently wore a crown on his head along with a red cape trimmed in ermine, bandoliers crisscrossing his chest, and two guns at his side, a shotgun on his left hip and a .45 on his right hip. Sometimes he even arrived at his dances being carried aloft on a gilded throne by his posse. He was known to fire his guns into the air at his shows in a display of his prowess as well as when he liked a song. He even occasionally played with a live grenade. He hosted a radio show on RJR called *Treasure Isle Time*, on which he always played the most current American hits, which he purchased on his trips to the United States. From 1956 to 1959, Reid was the "King of Sound and Blues," known for the rare, even exclusive 78-rpm tunes he played at the sound system dances. One of Reid's deejays and toasters was U-Roy, who later became a great reggae artist.

Coxsone Dodd, born in 1932, also had a family liquor store to promote, at the corner of Love Lane and Beeston Street, so he combined that effort with his love for jazz music, which he developed at a young age. While working in his mother's restaurant, Nanny's Corner, which later became the liquor store at Lawes Street and Ladd Lane, Coxsone heard the biggest jazz hits from America on his mother's radio. "My mother ran a liquor store at Beeston Street and Love Lane and I had a Morphy-Richards radio at her establishment," recalls Dodd. "In those days thirty watts was a whole heap of sound. I would stay in my room and play stuff like Fats Navarro, Dizzy Gillespie, Coleman Hawkins Illinois Jacquet, and Charlie Parker. Guys would hang out in the store and out on the piazza. Maybe have some drinks but a lot of food was sold too. When I arrived on the scene it was because I played jazz, and my followers could execute the dance for the sound I played" (quoted in Wilson, 2006, liner notes to *Bonanza Ska*). Coxsone loved this music. When he traveled to the United States to pick sugar cane in the southern states during the early 1950s, he shipped boxes full of records, speakers, a turntable, and a receiver back to Kingston. He was also skilled as a carpenter, learning to build from his father, who helped to construct the Carib Theatre and other theaters on the island, and he built his own giant speakers for his Downbeat sound system. Coxsone's sound was so popular that on any one night he would have up to four sound system dances in operation at various locations throughout Kingston. "I started to travel out. I exposed more tunes to the island than anybody else, songs by Billy Eckstine and Sarah Vaughn. They were on 78s. My friend Blackie would perform dance steps to show the crowd. He would do it right," says Dodd (Chris Wilson, liner notes to *Bonanza Ska*.

Vincent "King" Edwards, inspired by the success of his good friend Duke Reid, established his own sound system in 1955. Edwards, a ruthless operator, ruled like his mentor, using his henchmen to crash his rivals' dances and "flop" the competition. His system was called The Giant. He traveled frequently to the United States for the latest American R&B and at one time had up to seven sets playing around Kingston. In 1961, Edwards went into the recording business for a short time, recording The Skatalites, Baba Brooks, Sir Lord Comic, Lester Sterling, Eric "Monty" Morris, Bobby Aitken, Laurel Aitken, Shenley Duffus, and The Charmers before turning to politics in the mid-1960s, when he became a member of parliament.

Sound system dances were hugely popular with the masses who longed to escape the poverty and oppression that were rife in Kingston in the 1950s. When Duke Reid, Coxsone, or any number of sound system operators had their selectors spin the latest songs from America, hordes of people packed the indoor dance halls, such as the Cho Co Mo, Red Rooster, or the Pioneer, as well as open-air locations, lawns, that were fenced in to contain the crowd. At one point Maxfield Avenue alone had fourteen dance halls. Whoever could attract the most people sold the most liquor and made the most money, so sound system operators traveled to cities like Nashville, Memphis, New York, New Orleans, Miami, and Chicago and visited record stores like Randy's Records in Gallatin, Tennessee, and Rainbow Records in Harlem on a regular basis to buy the latest tunes. They played songs from American R&B artists like Ben E. King, The Impressions, and those on the Motown label. Other vendors set up stands outside the sound system dances and capitalized on the opportunity as well, selling ice-cold Red Stripe beer, fruit juice, curried goat, salt fish with callaloo, and spiced buns. Admission to the sound system dance was typically about two shillings on a Saturday night and five shillings on a holiday.

The sound system was crucial to spreading the music to the people, giving them a form of entertainment to raise their oppressed spirits. "I have heard it put that the sound system was your community radio station," writes historian Garth White, "because given the fact that many people, or most people couldn't afford the equipment to play music, and quite probably, weren't satisfied with the fare that the radio was offering, the sound system took up this role of providing music and entertainment for the people who could not afford to enjoy music in this way, outside of this sound system. . . . It is different when you compare it to other countries in the world, where music was listened to at home, or in the concert or stage show presentation in the US case, at house parties, but nowhere have I seen where you have this large outdoor gathering which is being serenaded by a sound system."

There was competition between sound system operators, and each had his followers. The competition was so aggressive that henchmen from each sound system's entourage were known to raid a competitor's dance, destroy his equipment, and literally break the needle from his turntable. Groups of rude boys, or gangs of thugs, were also known to align themselves with a sound system operator and defend his turf from opposing rude boys. Rude boys were disenfranchised youth in Kingston, who sometimes were simply mischievous, but at other times were downright violent. Garth White describes a rude boy as a "person, native, who is totally disenchanted with the ruling system; who generally is descended from the 'African' elements in the lower class and who is now armed with ratchets (German-made knives), other cutting instruments and with increasing frequency nowadays with guns and explosives" (White, 1967, p. 39). White notes that rude boys had similar possessions, such as shoes, hats, music, and stripped motorbikes, which served to bind them together in a community. Rude boys committed minor misdemeanors, such as jumping on the back of a streetcar for a free ride, but at other times they were much more violent and committed severe crimes such as murdering fellow rude boys or innocent schoolgirls. Well-known rude boy gangs were the Charles Street Spanglers, Phoenix, Skull, and Vikings.

Keeping the integrity of the sound system operator's own musical selections was crucial so competitors would not also play the same song, stealing the crowds to attend their dances instead and selling their drinks to the paying people. Sound system operators had theme songs exclusive to their sound, which were actually American R&B tunes they renamed for their use. Duke Reid's theme was "My Mother's Eyes" by Tab Smith. Coxsone Dodd's theme was "Later for Gator" by Willis Jackson, which he renamed "Coxsone's Hop." Operators engaged in sound system clashes, attempting to steal away the crowds using their rare R&B tunes, unless a rival found the same song and then played it repeatedly until it lost its appeal. This was known as killing the tune or flopping the competition.

Chris Wilson (2006) describes one of these face-offs:

> Rivalry between the sound systems led to one of the greatest showdowns of the Ska era. Coxsone and Duke Reid got together and along with their followers marched from Bond Street to Forresters Hall, while Prince Buster, shirtless and blowing a horn, and his followers marched up King Street to Jubilee where he joined the Supertown sound system. Jubilee being about 150 yards away from Forresters Hall made this one of the greatest sound clashes of all time. Who won is still hotly debated to this day, with some holding that Prince Buster came out on the top while others proclaim Sir Coxsone and Duke Reid the victors. But this is just an example of the high esteem that these sound systems were held in by their followers.

So that rival spies couldn't see their exclusive records, sound system operators scratched the names from the labels of their coveted songs, typically using a coin, or better yet, they made songs, exclusive songs, one-offs, specials, all their own. But that new endeavor required a recording studio, and key to that process were Ken Khouri and Graeme Goodall at Federal Records, the recording studio used by all early producers before the Marley family bought the structure in 1981 and renamed it Tuff Gong Recording Studio.

Goodall built a concert studio and used his own intuition and creativity to advance the industry. "I converted the men's lavatory into an echo chamber, which was quite interesting," he says. In addition, he built a "primitive studio" in the back of a furniture store on King Street owned by Ken Khouri, who at that time was in a franchise business importing music from Mercury Records in the United States. Khouri previously had a record label, Times Records, which distributed calypso tunes. Goodall says, "The only other person who was making records at that time was Stanley Motta and you couldn't really call it making records, although I guess it was making records because he was cutting the record disc, but Ken Khouri wanted to do something a little bit better so I advised him. He got a mic recorder, a tape recorder, some microphones and I threw a studio together for him and so he started making records. Ken Khouri and his wife Gloria, they were the principal owners of Federal Records. Actually, it started off as Records Limited up on King Street" (July 13, 2011).

Stanley Motta was a salesman who dealt in radio and electrical wares. He had a primitive studio behind his store that featured two microphones and had walls lined with carpet remnants to deaden the acoustics. Motta recorded mento music in 1951 and 1952 and sent the recordings to England to be mastered and pressed into 78-rpm shellac records at Decca by way of Emil Shallit's Melodisc company.

THE RECORDING INDUSTRY IGNITES

In the mid-1950s, music in the United States started to change. Rhythm and blues began to evolve into rock 'n' roll. Although Jamaicans frequently looked to the States for inspiration, they still craved their R&B and they did not like the new sound coming from the United States. "Rock 'n' roll was fine for the children of the Land of the Free, with their newly slicked-back hair, but in Kingston it was a disaster," write Laurence Cane-Honeysett and Michael de Koningh. "Dancers simply did not like the new hillbilly bop purveyed by Carl Perkins et al. and thirsted for the greasier shuffle of Bill Doggett and Nappy Brown" (2003, p. 21). There was an enormous demand for new music to compete at the sound system dances, but with the source of that music in the United States drying up, the solution to fulfilling that demand became obvious—record it in Jamaica from the pool of local talent.

Duke Reid was one of the first producers to record his own tunes so he could play them at his dances and on his radio show. The first song he recorded in 1958 on his own label, Trojan, was a 78-rpm mento tune from

Lord Power called "Penny Reel," which Eric "Monty" Morris later re-corded in 1964 for Reid's Treasure Isle label as a ska version. Other pro-ducers soon followed suit. Using primitive recording equipment, much of it made by hand, artists had one chance to get the tune right, and the musicians were frequently session artists who performed on song after song for the producer. As a result, the artists never really had the oppor-tunity to work together to rehearse or practice. Mistakes were made, but as long as they were small, the large crowds at the sound system dances wouldn't notice. Crowds only wanted to dance and have a good time.

Because Jamaican music up until this point was typically performed live for an audience or participants, the style of the recorded version of this music was engineered to reflect this public aspect of the music. Crowds wanted tunes that had a heavy beat, so recording engineers paid less attention to vocals and more attention to the driving rhythm and bass of the music. They put more emphasis on the lower frequencies. Goodall says, "My concept was these people want to dance to this music, they don't want to hear absolute one hundred percent clarity on a vocal. They want a driving music to dance to and this was in their soul and it was my job to somehow capture that in the studio and put it onto an acetate" (July 13, 2011).

Coxsone Dodd began recording at Federal Records as early as 1956. A few years later, all of the major sound system operators had turned pro-ducer, and they too were using Federal. One of the first songs from this era was Laurel Aitken's "Boogie in My Bones," a Jamaican creation that emulated the shuffling U.S. R&B style. Aitken came directly from the roots of Jamaica, using his vocal talents as a young boy to make a living. He took his special blend to the stage, working on cruise ships in King-ston Harbor as a teenager. When Aitken was only fifteen years old, he won the "Vere Johns Opportunity Hour," which made him very market-able in the tourist trade. "I used to play for the Jamaican Tourist Board. I used to sing and welcome the tourists coming from other countries in a big hut—you know, the calypso huts? And pretty loud colored shirts and sing them 'Welcome to Jamaica.' That's what I used to do. Then I used to sing at night at a club called the Colony Club and I used to sing calypso there, so I am coming from the roots of Jamaican music," says Aitken (1997 interview). When he recorded his first song, "Boogie in My Bones," in 1958 for the wealthy white producer Chris Blackwell, Aitken's career was solidified. Goodall engineered this song in the studio, placing em-phasis on the kick drum and string bass and carefully placing the micro-phones to produce the driving sound the dance crowds craved. Jamaican dancers needed to feel the vibe of the music, the pounding in the chest, in the bones, more than to see the composition.

Many of the Jamaican recordings during these years were cover songs of popular American R&B tunes. Bandleader and trombonist Carlos Mal-colm recalls, "In the early '60s, to meet the appetite for blues-oriented music among Jamaican youth (who listened constantly to music from New Orleans and Miami, FL), Jamaican producers turned from importing 45 rpm 7 [inch] blues records from the U.S. to doing 'covers' of them with local bands and renaming the covers. For instance, I remember 'Guns Fever' by Baba Brooks was a cover of a song named 'My Shawl' played by Xavier Cugat and his Orchestra in a movie named 'Easy to Love' featuring the swimming queen, Esther Williams" (2011). Other covers include Floyd Dixon's "Hey Bartender," covered by Laurel Aitken, which has a beat close to ska, but instead is that shuffling style adopted from the States; Ray Charles's "Swanee River Rock," covered by Clue J & The Blues Blasters; Louis Jordan's huge hit "Caledonia," recorded by Lord Lebby as well as Val Bennett; and "Saffronia B" by Calvin Boze, covered by Lloyd Charmers. Jamaican vocalists like Laurel Aitken, Al T. Joe, Derrick Morgan, Owen Gray, and Bunny & Skully cut their chops on R&B with their own creations.

All recordings during the late 1950s were for mass consumption at the sound system dances. Only the wealthy owned record players in those days, so listening to the local talent could only happen at the live performances at the theaters or at the dance halls. But it wasn't long before these well-trained jazz musicians, who esteemed the R&B of America, stopped repeating the songs desired by the tourists and producers and started to develop a music more akin to their own tastes, a voice of the people, a blend of all that had come before. This music brought together the jazz of the clubs, the R&B of the yards, the drums of Africa, the mento and calypso, and indigenous forms in all their sound and display. This music was ska.

THREE

Freedom Sound

Critics of the newly emergent ska in the early 1960s at first described it as "one of the most monotonous and unimaginative rhythms of all time," which went "oompha-oompha-oompha from the beginning to the end of an evening." Granted, some artists lacked the technique and background to take it to the next level. But other artists, trained at Alpha Boys School or in the clubs and studios during the 1950s, gave ska music a brilliance that established it forever as a genuine genre, with merit, significance, and importance.

SKA

Ask any Jamaican today what ska is and he or she will call it "the oldies." Some younger generations might not even be able to tell you what it is at all. But without ska, no rocksteady, no reggae, no dub or dancehall or even Bob Marley himself would have emerged. The instrumentalists, because of their high caliber, pushed the quality of the vocalists. What gives ska its distinctive sound is the rhythm, a strong section of horns, and a peppy tempo to get the crowd moving. Vocalist Laurel Aitken, "Godfather of Ska" explains: "You mix calypso and rhythm and blues and just play the guitar, just shuffle the guitar like the American does with rhythm and blues. Not today's rhythm and blues, but the rhythm and blues forty years ago. You know that shufflin' guitar? Well that's ska. No one anybody started doing that, but it was a good flavor. It flavored the way people were dancing in those days, so in a way, ska just came" (1997 interview). Guitarist Ernest Ranglin has described the difference between the R&B beat and the ska beat as *chink*-ka, *chink*-ka, *chink*-ka in R&B versus ka-*chink*, ka-*chink*, ka-*chink* in ska. And of course, the presence of horns, a healthy brass section to both punctuate the sound for rhythmic value as well as carry the melodies and harmonies, is essential to the sound.

Certainly it wasn't the first time a rhythm had ever been syncopated to stress the two and four beats instead of the one and the three in a typical quarter-note measure. Memphis pianist Roscoe Gordon did it in 1952 with his tune, "No More Doggin'," and decades before that, in 1927, New Orleans–born jazz pianist and bandleader Richard M. Jones and the Jazz Wizards did it with "African Hunch," complete with vocalized peps, percussive tisking to punctuate the tune, and "Boar Hog Blues." But when Jamaican musicians blended this beat with their own concoction of jazz, R&B, calypso, and mento, along with the desperate need to eke out a living in an oppressive yet newly independent country full of expectations, the result was electrifying.

The first ska song, most agree, was "Easy Snappin'," by pianist Theophilus Beckford, produced by Coxsone Dodd in 1959 on his original Worldisc label. The song was hugely popular and even sold well in England when it was released there. This song represents the ska sound in its earliest years, but it wasn't until about 1961 and 1962 that the sound flourished in the studios.

What most musicians do not agree on is the first person or group of people to create the ska sound. Many artists and producers claim to have been the first. It is a battle not unlike the boasting stick fights of carnival. Drummer Lloyd Knibb says, "I am the originator of the ska beat also. In the studio, me and Coxsone Downbeat try out a beat. My beat sound different, heavier, so my drumming is distinct. So most all the drummers try to play like me. They like the beat but then can't get it to sound like me. So that is how it started" (1997 interview). Dodd has said it was he who asked Ernest Ranglin to try the offbeat with his guitar. Producer and vocalist Prince Buster asserts that it was he who created the style. He says that drummer Arkland "Drumbago" Parks, who was also a music arranger, was essential to this process. He claims to have asked Drumbago to play a march, a style of song that Prince Buster favored even as a young child, the same style of music that was played during carnival and in processions, heavy with drums. Prince Buster says he asked Drumbago to stress the offbeat, guitarist Jah Jerry to perform a guitar strum, and Dennis Campbell to perform saxophone syncopation to accent the rhythm, thus creating the ska sound. Carlos Malcolm claims the ska beat was just a mistake as Jamaican musicians tried to play the American R&B but the indigenous beat crept in.

The name of the music itself, "ska," also has the same ownership issues. Prince Buster also claims to have coined this word, saying it was an abbreviation of the word "scatter," a command he was giving to his competitors, Duke Reid and Coxsone, when he was proclaiming his prowess. Bassist Lloyd Brevett says it was either the sound of the guitar or a term from a jazzy hip-cat phrase thrown around the studio by a musician: "We started to change the beat. We started to play ska, but we never really name it. But we play ska. Guitar, 'ska, ska, ska.' One guy come to the studio used to come to the studio used to say, 'Wha-up, Skavoovie?' That guy was Cluett Johnson, bass player, joking guy. 'Wha-up, Skavoovie?' He came there so regular and talk skavoovie, that together with the guitar, 'ska, ska, ska,' that name the music ska. Yeah. That is it" (1997 interview).

IN THE STUDIO

To earn a few pounds, musicians gathered outside studios where producers auditioned young talent or had their scouts screen the musicians. Producer Leslie Kong had his scout, artist extraordinaire Derrick Morgan, audition talent and recommend the best, which is how James Chambers, the singer better known as Jimmy Cliff, got his start. Boys with no skills came to try their hand at singing, backed up by studio musicians who made the rounds of the studios, signing contracts to work exclusively for each producer but honoring none. The studios in the late 1950s and early 1960s, owned by Duke Reid, Coxsone, Leslie Kong, Justin Yap, Randy Chin, and others, were solely for auditioning and practicing, what little practicing they did. All recording was done at Federal Records.

Federal Records was founded by Ken Khouri, who was born in Kingston, the son of a Cuban mother and Lebanese father. His family was in the dry goods and furniture business, so Khouri grew up in a family that worked hard, and he learned how to make a living in business. He learned about music as a kid, working for the Issa family, friends of his family. The Issas owned jukeboxes all over the island, and after Khouri bought a disc recorder from a friend while in Miami, he entered the recording industry for the first time.

Khouri first began recording calypsos, traveling around the island to various nightclubs to record the performances. He had the masters made in England and records made at Decca, 78s of Lord Flea. But this process took lots of time, and there were no other options in Jamaica because the island had no facilities for pressing records. So Khouri traveled to California and purchased the equipment he needed to set up his own plant. He established his first label, Times Records, named after the Times Variety Store on King Street, where he sold the calypso records. Khouri recorded the songs from a studio that he built with his wife Gloria at 129 King Street. It was the first studio and pressing plant on the island, built in 1947. According to Khouri, his plant was built prior to those built by Stanley Motta and Dada Tewari (Katz 2004). In 1954, Khouri started the Pioneer Company, which worked with franchises like Mercury in the United States. In 1957, he officially started Federal Records, moving to an industrial area on Marcus Garvey Drive.

Federal Records engineer Graeme Goodall says Federal wasn't only used because it was the only choice, but also because producers could have an acetate cut quickly, for a dance that night. "There [were] no other engineers, there [were] no other facilities. There was no Studio One studio. Eventually Downbeat did actually build a studio, but that was well into it and he only really built it because Duke Reid wanted to build one too," says Goodall (February 8, 2013). Studio One at 13 Brentford Road, which had a one-track board, did not open until 1965, and Duke Reid's recording studio only opened in 1967. Until then, both producers used Federal Records like everyone else and used their own locations as audition space and for liquor sales. "At Federal Records they came because here was a place where they could walk in with an artist and a nucleus of studio musicians. They came in on their particular days to cut discs," Goodall says (July 13, 2011). Music producers in those early days were like film producers—they sponsored the production, organized those involved to make it happen, and paid for it up front, reaping the rewards on the back end for the life of the song, because there was no such thing as royalties or artist copyrights.

NO ROYALTIES

Around 1962, ska music was in full swing. With producers recording up to ten sides a day, they used the songs to reap the rewards of fame and cash from liquor sales. Music production was a factory system. Artists either punched in and out on a time clock or were paid by the record side, about £2 a tune if they were lucky. There were no royalties. Even today, the royalties are owned by the producers and their estates, so those whose talent and imagination created the songs, like Don Drummond and Roland Alphonso and even Bob Marley in his earliest years, either don't see a dime or receive a small slice of the pie from reworked agreements. For example, on one of Bob Marley's first songs, a ska song called "Simmer Down," because he recorded the song for Studio One in 1964, only Marley's estate and Coxsone Dodd's estate receive royalties, and they fought in court in the 1990s for profits from the song. None of the artists who perform the music on this song, which sold eighty thousand copies in the first few months following its release—not Roland Alphonso on saxophone, nor Lloyd Knibb on drums, nor Lloyd Brevett on bass, nor Don Drummond on trombone, nor Tommy McCook on saxophone, nor any of the others, not even The Wailers, who sing backup, Peter Tosh, Bunny Livingston, Junior Braithwaite, and Beverley Kelso—get one red cent from "Simmer Down." Marley's widow, Rita Marley, said she had never received money from any of Marley's early work with Coxsone. This is but one of hundreds, even thousands of songs, earning hundreds, even thousands of dollars, for their producers' estates. Producers defend their exploitation by saying that it was the system of the day, akin to today's "free culture" of ripping tracks from a torrent or mega-upload music site.

THE SKATALITES

To "get a little piece of the action" and establish themselves as more than just studio musicians, a group of hornsmen and vocalists decided to form their own band, The Skatalites. Without The Skatalites, ska would have been relegated to an embryonic form of other genres, or an "oomp-pah, oomp-pah, oomp-pah" without feeling, according to some music critics of the time. Because of The Skatalites, ska became a genre in its own right.

The members of The Skatalites were leader Tommy McCook, tenor saxophone and flute; Don Drummond, trombone; Roland Alphonso, tenor saxophone; Lester Sterling, alto saxophone; Johnny "Dizzy" Moore, trumpet; Lloyd Brevett, double bass; Lloyd Knibb, drums; Jerome "Jah Jerry" Haynes, guitar; and Donat Roy "Jackie" Mittoo, piano. The name The Skatalites was a play on the word "satellites," because the space race was under way. Their first gig was in May 1964 in Rae Town at the Hi-Hat Club, although the musicians had been performing in the studio together for years. From gig to gig, studio to studio, other musicians would filter in and out of the group, such as guitarists Ernest Ranglin, Harold McKenzie, and Lyn Taitt; vocalist Lord Tanamo; trumpeters Oswald "Baba" Brooks and Rupert Dillon; and drummer Arkland "Drumbago" Parks, among others. Performing on stage and in the studio, The Skatalites were accompanied by four vocalists, although much of their repertoire was instrumental, in the same theme and variation style of its jazz forefather. One of the vocalists, Doreen Shaffer, remembers, "At that time, when the band was formed, we had four vocalists, I being the only female. You have Jackie Opel, Lord Tanamo, you have Tony DaCosta, and myself" (1997 interview).

Many of the members of The Skatalites were graduates of Alpha Boys School: Don Drummond, Lester Sterling, Johnny "Dizzy" Moore, and Tommy McCook. Lester Sterling recalls the days when they first came together: "When we reach teenage days, we all meet, young musicians, talkin' and make arrangement to practice together. We have jam sessions. Don Drummond was there back then. Don Drummond used to play with us as a kid, and Roland, Jah Jerry, Ernest Ranglin, all these practiced" (1997 interview). The Skatalites recorded hit songs for all producers of the day, especially for the two who gave them all their first opportunity as young musicians, Coxsone Dodd and Duke Reid. Roland Alphonso says, "When the band started, we were playing for Coxsone. The band were Coxsone's musicians and make records for him" (1997 interview). They also recorded for producers like Justin Yap, Vincent "King" Edwards,

Prince Buster, Leslie Kong, Lindon and Sonia Pottinger, and Vincent "Randy" Chin. They performed at many clubs around Kingston, such as the Silver Slipper Club, the Yacht Club, Club Havana, the Blinking Beacon, Wicky Wacky, and the Sombrero Club. They performed throughout Jamaica, at clubs in Montego Bay like the Wooden Spoon, Cellar Club, and the Embassy Club, and eighteen miles away from Montego Bay in Falmouth at Good Hope and Club Calypso. But they had a residency at the Bournemouth Club in south Kingston, performing regularly on Wednesday, Friday, and Saturday nights, as well as at the Orange Bowl on Sunday nights.

The talent of these musicians pressured the vocalists to perform at an even higher level. Garth White claims:

> Although you can hear the potential in someone like Bob Marley and an Alton [Ellis] and a Toots [Hibbert]. In some of these early recordings you can almost visualize the music pushing them to perform. Well, look at [S]immer Down, that introduction [by Don Drummond]. Anybody singing after that introduction has to come good. And then the humility of Roland [Alphonso] on the solo, where he doesn't try to dominate. It's a laid back solo that fits in with the theme of simmering down. And this is Roland who is another virtuoso . . . and that only comes from competent people who are confident of their abilities. (White, 2007, p. 91–92)

Elements of Latin music crept into The Skatalites' catalog that they performed for all the producers in town. Their collection of songs contained both subtle Latin rhythms as well as more overt covers of Latin songs from the likes of Mongo Santamaria. Having members of The Skatalites like Tommy McCook enter the band fresh off the boat from his contracted job in Nassau, Bahamas, where he played mambos, cha-chas, and bossa novas, surely influenced their sound. Roland Alphonso, who was born in Cuba, also brought in flavors of his own.

WAREIKA HILLS

Many of the musicians in The Skatalites performed for their own fulfillment in the Wareika Hills, where they learned the rhythms of the Burru and Rasta, as well as the doctrines. What was known as the Far East sound came to ska through the Wareika Hills, the sound that gave birth to reggae.

Oswald Williams, or Count Ossie, was the leader of his Rasta bredren at a camp, similar to other leaders like Leonard P. Howell and Mortimer Planno. Count Ossie was a drummer who learned from the Burru. The Burru and Rasta were both ostracized by society and tormented by the government from the 1930s through the 1970s, so they naturally came together to live in peace. The Rastafari gained the music of the Burru, and the Burru gained the spirituality of the Rastafari. Musicians who came to the hills to play and smoke vibed off the drumming, which became part of their performance. The sound became part of popular music in Jamaica. "Besides lawyers, doctors, and 'Indian chiefs,' Ossie's camps attracted the cream of Jamaican jazz and pop musicians, including the Gaynairs, Tommy McCook, Viv Hall, Don Drummond, Ernest Ranglin, and even musicians from abroad. It was during these sessions of reasoning and music coming together that the compatibility of Rasta drumming and voice instruments and the creative excitement in the interchange were realized. It is said that it was out of this experience that the trombone of the great Don D (Drummond) took wing," writes historian Verena Reckord (1982, p. 76).

Producer Prince Buster, seeking to capitalize on this sound, asked Count Ossie and his drummers to record for him in 1960 on the song "Oh, Carolina" by the Folkes Brothers. Kevin O'Brien Chang and Wayne Chen note in *Reggae Routes* that "in time, Count Ossie developed a significant reputation and eventually Prince Buster, then a singer–set deejay–cum–producer in search of a 'different sound,' decided to try some of Ossie's rhythms in the studio. With the three youthful Folkes Brothers on vocals, Ossie and his drummers providing an African cross-rhythmic accompaniment and contrasting American style piano, Buster produced arguably the most famous, influential and important of early Jamaican records, 'Oh Carolina'" (1998, p. 27).

Genius musician Don Drummond, who played trombone for The Skatalites, is credited for creating this sound and is also responsible for composing all of the group's original tunes. Tommy McCook may have been the bandleader, but Drummond was the spine of the group, despite his frequent departures due to his mental health struggles. Drummond learned the themes of his music not at Alpha Boys School where he studied as a young boy, not in the wealthy tourist clubs where he performed during the jazz years, and not even in the studio where he tried to make a living, but in the Wareika Hills where he and other musicians, like Tommy McCook, Rico Rodriguez, Lloyd Knibb, and others, joined together in musical communion. There they played with Count Ossie and his drummers, the Mystic Revelation of the Rastafari, as well as the Rastafarian brothers, sisters, and youth who lived at the camp, during the nyabinghi—drumming, chanting, reasoning, and dancing—or when they would come up to the hills for a smoke after a show. Don Drummond combined his use of minor chords and a sorrowful feel with themes he learned in the hills to compose songs with titles like "Far East," "The Reburial of Marcus Garvey," "Addis Ababa," and "Marcus Junior." This was the sound, the ethic, the spirit, that became part of the reggae revolution.

"Count Ossie was a Rastafarian and the main thing the Rastafarian element brought to Jamaica and to Jamaican music was a real recognition and honour of Africa," says Chris Blackwell. "In American black music there was nothing at that time that was embracing the African heritage, there was very little notion then in America of Afrocentricity. In Jamaica, though, there was a section of the population that was looking to the west and listening to Miami and New Orleans radio, but also there existed the Rastafarian element which was saying that Jamaicans should hang on to our cultural roots. This has been a key dynamic in Jamaican music" (quoted in O'Brien and Chang, p. 28).

SKA PRODUCERS

There was plenty of money to be made in Jamaica. Coxsone and Duke Reid were not the only producers recording ska music, and The Skatalites were not the only band making records. Some producers, like Coxsone and Reid, were ruthless at times and could be unfair and exploitative, but without them ska music would never have had the necessary mouthpiece to communicate to the people and the world.

One of the very influential ska producers of the 1960s was Leslie Kong, also known as Beverley's after the name of the restaurant, ice cream parlor, and upstairs real estate office he owned with his two brothers, Fats and Cecil, on the corner of North and Orange Streets. The enterprising Leslie decided to pursue a career in recording after he discovered Jimmy Cliff, who had penned a song to flatter the prosperous Kong, called "Dearest Beverley." Kong also gave another newbie his start, recording two songs in 1962 that were a first for the young Robert Nesta Marley: "One Cup of Coffee" and "Judge Not."

When he was just twelve years old, Lloyd "The Matador" Daley built his first radio set, which he converted into a sound system. He named his sound system "The Matador" and began recording for himself on his labels, Matador and Mystic. Hi-Lite, whose real name was Simeon L. Smith, had a record shop at the corner of Spanish Town Road and Harris Street that was also a hat shop, hardware store, and (in common with so many other producers) liquor store. He founded the Smith's label and started working with musicians in his store, then took them to Federal to record.

Justin Yap and his brother Duke Yap ran the Top Deck label. Justin Yap was introduced to The Skatalites by Allan "Bim Bim" Scott, Coxsone's assistant, who knew the musicians personally and suggested Yap record them. During a now-famous all-night recording session using Studio One in November 1964, Yap recorded some of The Skatalites' classic tunes, all written by Don Drummond, including "Confucius," "Chinatown," "The Reburial," "Smiling," and "Marcus Junior." Musicians loved recording for Yap, because he paid more than other producers and always paid in cash, not with a check. He, like Vincent Chin and Leslie

Kong, was known to be honest and treated musicians with respect, something hard to come by among Jamaican producers.

Vincent "Randy" Chin began his foray into the music industry as a teenager in the 1950s during the heyday of R&B. Working for Isaac Issa, a jukebox owner (like Chris Blackwell), Chin was responsible for removing the old 45s and replacing them with the newest, hottest tunes. Chin asked Issa if he could keep the discards, which Issa allowed for a small fee. In 1958, Chin opened up his own store, selling the records and making a profit. He named his store after Randy's Record Shop of Gallatin, Tennessee, which sponsored an American R&B radio show that Jamaicans could receive on the island. With a taste for the musical life, Randy began producing, and he recorded all of the greats during his days in the business. He continued the label into the reggae years, and his son, Clive Chin, runs the label, which today is called VP Records.

One of the more important producers of the day was Cecil Bustamante Campbell, or Prince Buster, who started his career in music after he was hired to be a henchman for Coxsone. Buster's job for Coxsone was to help identify the musicians who performed on the competition's records at sound system dances by befriending and then betraying them. Prince Buster did this first to Tom "the Great" Sebastian, who ran a sound system but quickly got out of the competitive business because it was so ruthless, and in 1971 he committed suicide. Prince Buster used to work in Sebastian's record store and betrayed him to Coxsone. While working for Coxsone, Prince Buster, despite growing up with Duke Reid's friends, broke Reid's record needle at a dance one night trying to ruin him, which caused Prince Buster strife in the neighborhood.

Before long, Prince Buster bit the hand that fed him and betrayed Coxsone, too. When Prince Buster heard that Duke Reid had obtained a copy of Coxsone's exclusive song, "Later for Gator," by Willis "Gatortail" Jackson, which Coxsone used as his theme song and renamed "Coxsone's Hop," Prince Buster convinced reluctant Coxsone to go to Kingston's Jubilee Hall for a show. When Reid played Coxsone's exclusive theme song, Coxsone is said to have hit the floor in shock, dropping his Red Stripe beer. It was after this that Prince Buster, who had no loyalties to anyone but himself, started his own sound system and label, The Voice of the People, recording artists like The Skatalites, the Folkes Brothers, and of course, himself. Ken Khouri at Federal Records banned Prince Buster from recording because he rarely paid his fees on time and tried to finagle his charges, but Graeme Goodall defended him. Prince Buster was able to record many of his own classic ska songs, such as "Madness," "One Step Beyond," and "Al Capone." After meeting Muhammad Ali, Prince Buster joined the Nation of Islam and now goes by his stage name as well as Muhammed Yusef Ali.

Ska history frequently overlooks the importance of women during this era, perhaps because there were so few involved. The industry and culture were male dominated. To understand the climate for women in 1950s–1960s Jamaica, one need only look as far as the songs themselves. Women were appealed to as subjects of love in the tradition of American R&B. Their beauty was hailed, from "Miss Jamaica," to "Fat Girl in Red." But women were also the objects of sexual desire, either overtly or through innuendo, or they were the desirers, as in Jackie Opel's classic "Push Wood." They were gossipers, meddlers, wrongdoers, like those found in Justin Hinds and the Dominoes' "Rub Up Push Up" or "Jezebel." They were inept, as in Desmond Dekker's "Get Up Edina," and disobedient to man, so they needed Prince Buster's "10 Commandments." They were also abused, as in The Two Kings' "Hit You Let You Feel It," whose B side is perplexingly "Honey I Love You."

Viewed in this context, it is even more impressive to realize the influence a handful of women have had on the Jamaican music industry, and perhaps none as great as producer Sonia Pottinger. After getting her foot in the door when her husband, Lindon O. Pottinger, founded the Tip Top Record Shop and recording studio, Sonia took control of the reins when the two parted ways in the mid-1960s. Sonia built her own studio and pressing plant behind the Tip Top shop to support her three children and a fourth child born in the early 1970s. But beyond financial need, Sonia had a heart for the music, a feel and intuition that brought her recording and production company to new heights for her artists.

Going solo in 1965, Sonia Pottinger decided to try her hand at production and recorded "Every Night" by Joe White & Chuck Josephs, backed by the Baba Brooks Band, before going on to establish her own labels: Gay Feet, Excel, Pep, and High Note, and an imprint called Glory, which released gospel titles.

Sonia recorded fellow female artist Millicent "Patsy" Todd, one of the few females recording alone at the time. Two of the solo songs that Sonia produced for Patsy were "Fire in Your Wire" and "Pata Pata Rock Steady," which had unique content. "Fire in Your Wire" is a soca tune originally written by Calypso Rose of Tobago, another pioneering woman, whose lyrics are the typical sexual innuendo of calypso and soca, but certainly not typical of those sung by a female up to that point. "Pata Pata Rock Steady" was also written by a female artist, Dorothy Masuka, for singer Miriam Makeba, both South Africans. Sonia had an affinity for African music, especially African drums, so she brought in Count Ossie's drummers for the track.

During the rocksteady era (1967 to 1968), Sonia Pottinger's career really began to thrive. She produced and promoted numerous female artists, male artists, and groups. In the 1970s, Sonia continued her support for strong women artists like Judy Mowatt, Lorna Bennett, Phyllis Dillon, Carlene Davis, and Sonya Spence. Her long list of male artists and groups included performers such as U Roy, Big Youth, and of course, Culture. They came to Mrs. P, as they called her, because she was honest and didn't exploit them; she paid more than others; and brought something no one else in the business on the island had—woman's intuition. But even though Sonia Pottinger was a record producer on a par with others of the day, she was not given the same respect, one would assume, because the industry and culture were so male dominated.

SKA FEUDS

Like the stick fights of carnival and the competition between sound system operators and their henchmen, ska artists also had their battles, sometimes playful, sometimes with a bit more edge. The first and most notorious of these feuds was between Prince Buster and Derrick Morgan.

Morgan (1997) reports that their feud started when he chose to record his song "Forward March" with Beverley's instead of Prince Buster. He says that Prince Buster also mistakenly thought that Morgan had stolen one of his studio instrumentalists, Headley Bennett, to do a solo in the song. So Prince Buster recorded a song in retaliation called "Blackhead Chinaman." Prince Buster's song was banned by RJR, Radio Jamaica, because of its racist content. It was a direct racist insult against Kong, Morgan's producer. Morgan fired back with "Blazing Fire," and each retaliated in kind, back and forth in song.

A major part of the Prince Buster and Derrick Morgan rivalry was expressed through their rudeboy and Judge Dread songs, which continued their musical stick fight and call-and-response antics. Songs like Derrick Morgan's "Tougher Than Tough" address rude boys directly, with a judge speaking at the beginning of the song to the gangsters brought in for using ratchets and throwing bombs. Their reply to the judge that "rudies don't fear" inspired the marginalized youth in Jamaica, who turned to crime and egged on Prince Buster, who responded with his Judge Dread songs. Judge Dread was a character in Prince Buster's songs who sentenced the rude boys, regardless of their pleas for mercy and even crying, to such unreasonable sentences as 400 years behind bars.

But the rivalry wasn't just musical. The fans of Morgan and Prince Buster were members of street gangs who engaged in violent fights. In Kingston bars, men fought and cut each other with knives in disputes over the two singers. Prime Minister Hugh Lawson Shearer decided to step in and quell the violence, so he approached the *Daily Gleaner*, the biggest newspaper in the country, for help. Shearer staged a photo of Prince Buster and Derrick Morgan shaking hands to prevent further violence in Kingston. The rivalry was not as friendly as it might seem in song, says Morgan (1997). Even when the two toured England together in 1963, Prince Buster paid audience members to boo Morgan's performances.

Musical feuds continued in Jamaica in the following years, between artists like Beenie Man and Bounty Killer, and Ninja Man and Shabba Ranks. Musical battles are a tradition found today in many genres, but perhaps most noticeably in hip-hop. Artists such as Common and Ice Cube, LL Cool J and KRS-One, Tupac Shakur and Notorious B.I.G., and Lil Kim and Nicki Minaj feud with each other in "beef" songs, a practice that began in ska and even long before, in Africa.

TOPICS OF SKA

Ska music is largely instrumental. However, there were some vocalists and vocal duos, who sang about the traditional topics found in American R&B songs, like love and relationships. The titles of ska songs also reflected politics abroad, such as The Skatalites' "Lee Harvey Oswald" and "Christine Keeler," as well as the political movements of the time that ska musicians discussed in the Wareika Hills Rasta camps, like black nationalism and biblical topics.

Themes also included references to American pop culture, specifically movies that were hugely popular in Jamaica, such as spaghetti Westerns with tough cowboy stereotypes and spy movies. "The Guns of Navarone" was a seminal hit for The Skatalites, as were the James Bond theme, "Dick Tracy," and "Lawless Street," which was made after the 1955 Western movie, while "007 (Shanty Town)" became a big hit for Desmond Dekker in later years. "Bonanza Ska" was a ska version of the classic television theme song, played by Carlos Malcolm and his outfit. "Duck Soup" by Baba Brooks was written in honor of the Marx Brothers' 1933 movie of the same name. "Such songs reveal the close affinities ska musicians felt to liminal male characters—tricksters, spies, cowboys, private dicks—as well as the ongoing media and commodity ties between Jamaica, Britain, and the United States," writes scholar Joseph Heathcott (2003, p. 195). Ska lyrics, akin to the boasting of stick fights, also proclaimed musical prowess. Everyone was the king of ska, the godfather of ska, the duke, the prince, boss, sir, in lyric after lyric. Similarly, sexual prowess, barely cloaked in innuendo, was also a commonality and a nod to calypso days, in songs like "Push Wood" by Jackie Opel, in which a woman begs Jackie by name for long wood to keep her fire hot. But there were also a number of very sweet love songs, akin to the teenager-in-love tunes from the states, the American R&B love songs. Many of the vocal duos included these lyrics, especially those by Derrick & Patsy or Stranger & Patsy.

Ska lyrics also acknowledged the struggles of everyday people in Jamaica. In "Starvation," Derrick Morgan sings about children with no shoes or food, and no employment; "Time Tough," by Toots & the Maytals, describes not being able to pay one's rent. They dreamed of a better life. "Ska songs also expressed youth aspirations and fantasies for a more glamorous and carefree lifestyle. Braggadocio was an early and important theme in the genre, as young men attempted to compensate for the alienation and dehumanization of shantytown life and labor. Typical of this variety was Don Drummond's egocentric 'Don Cosmic,' or Roland Alfonso's [sic] hopeful 'Streets of Gold'" (Heathcott, 2003, p. 195).

While Morgan and Prince Buster had their share of back-and-forth songs referencing rude boys and Judge Dread, there were plenty of rude boy songs that either supported the rude boy culture or denounced it. They reflected the violence of the times, asking youths to simmer down and put away their ratchets, or they glorified gangsters and stylized criminals, such as Prince Buster's "Al Capone," as well as "007 (Shanty Town)," "Rude Boy Train," and "Rudy Got Soul" by Desmond Dekker. But there were many more that warned about the rudeboy lifestyle: "Cry Tough" and "Dance Crasher" by Alton Ellis, "No Good Rudie" by Justin Hinds, "Cool Off Rudies" by Derrick Morgan, "Don't Be a Rude Boy" by the Rulers, and dozens of others.

There were also many songs about ska itself. Certainly the music that Byron Lee & the Dragonaires used to introduce the genre to the world at the New York World's Fair in 1964 had this theme; it was marketing, after all. "Jamaica Ska" was obviously about the music and dance. But there were others, like "Independence Ska" by The Skatalites, "I'm in the Mood for Ska" by Lord Tanamo, and "Ska All Over the World" by Jimmy Cliff, as well as silly mash-ups with the word ska, like "Skaravan" and "Ska Doo Da Ba" by The Skatalites, perhaps to play off of their own moniker's innovation.

It is important to note that even though many ska songs are instrumental, with no words to convey the message, the music still speaks of the sorrow of the people and the promise of the future. Musician and historian Myrna Hague-Bradshaw said of Jamaican jazz, "If you know the language, you hear the anger" (Cooke 2013), and the same can be said of Jamaican ska.

SKA COVERS

Not only did ska musicians cover movie themes, they also either completely hijacked other artists' songs or sampled them in an era before the rampant sampling that proliferated in the dancehall and hip-hop genres. The Skatalites have covered almost the entire *Watermelon Man* album by Mongo Santamaria, according to Skatalites manager Ken Stewart. Trombonist and bandleader Carlos Malcolm reveals that at the request of Coxsone, Don Drummond's "Far East" incorporated Judy Garland's "Trolley Song" from *Meet Me in St. Louis*, but in a different chord, so that it is less identifiable. The opening to The Skatalites "Occupation," written by Don

Drummond, is a blatant homage to a popular song of the day, Johnny Cash's "Ring of Fire." Barbie Gaye's "Lollipop" became a huge hit for Jamaican Millie Small, who recorded "My Boy Lollipop." A good number of mento and calypso songs were covered as well, such as Duke of Iron's" Big Bamboo," covered by Roland Alphonso, and Count Lasher's "Sally Brown," covered by Laurel Aitken. Sometimes cover songs incorporated a little play on words, such as Roland Alphonso's cover of Duke Ellington's "Caravan," "Skaravan"; Lord Tanamo's "I'm in the Mood for Ska," covering Fats Domino's "I'm in the Mood for Love"; and "Ska Boo Da Ba," The Skatalites' cover of Bill Doggett's "Boo Da Ba." The list of covers and ska witticisms is almost endless, as Jamaicans practiced their tradition of adopting other art forms, improving on them, and making them their own.

The Jamaican versions of other genres of music, the battles between artists, and the themes popular with the people helped to shape the identity of Jamaica's music. The music became so much a part of the fabric of the country that today Jamaicans with a strong pride in the music feel enraged that other cultures have borrowed it for their own, and they are suspicious of others' intentions. This paranoia exists because the music and the people are so intertwined. To fully see how the music became an integral part of the people's identity, one needs to consider not only the birth of the music, but the birth of the nation in the days and years following independence, when Jamaica was searching for its own distinctive character.

FOUR

Out of Many, One People

The sound system dances at which ska music was played gave Jamaicans a chance to escape from their struggle. For the working class, the only opportunity to earn a living was by laboring in the sugarcane fields, mining bauxite in the mineral pits, or hauling bananas from the forests. Labor and tourism were the only ways to earn a few pounds. Labor riots, strikes, and rebellions against the wealthy landowners and colonizers strove to bring rights to the peasant class. The shackles of European colonization were tight, so when the promise of a new future came, Jamaicans were full of hope.

On August 6, 1962, Jamaica became independent from Britain. It had been a long, but respectful, struggle against the colonizers. Jamaicans had won their freedom. They were finally free—from the slave trade that had wracked the country since the British inhabited the island in the mid-1600s and made their fortunes by exploiting men, women, and children stolen from Africa; from the political oppression of the British colonizers who controlled every facet of Jamaican life, from trade, to law, to development; and from the poverty that sent good men to the grave—or so they thought.

Jamaica was an expectant place after independence, ignited by the promise of the island's potential. Huge celebrations materialized in every town as Jamaicans took to the streets to dance and make merry with their neighbors and strangers alike. They were all one people now. Banners and flags flew from the facades of every building. Women prepared feasts of rice and peas, ox tail stew, and ackee and saltfish, now the national dish. Parades snaked through the streets.

There was a call for celebrations to represent the new national identity. *The Daily Gleaner* editor in chief Theodore Sealy appealed, "Let the people sing." He wrote:

Some people want lavish pageants. Others want prayer. Some think Jamaica should try to outdo and outspend everything that Africa and India has attempted or done—just to show how great we in Jamaica are. Others feel that the mood that should be left after the first Independence Day is not a mood of glory but a mood of gratitude at having lived to see the day. All these ideas and many more are now being talked about in the home, at clubs, in sunshacks, in yam fields, in bars, on the pavements, what should the government do? What should the people do? (Sealy, 1962, p. 6)

What the government did, and what the people did, were two very different things. The establishment and the people had two separate celebrations. This occurred in part because Jamaican society was, and still is to a large degree, stratified into upper and lower classes. The Institute of Social and Economic Research reported that "urban Kingston and St. Andrew consist of a highly class-stratified population in which most residential areas are class homogenous" (Stone, 1973, p. 34). Similarly, popular music during the time of Jamaica's independence fell into two categories, a reflection of Jamaican society: uptown and downtown. Dr. Basil Waine Kong writes, "We were told that if we didn't want to be second class, we had to speak and dress Western style, learn English manners, poetry, history and music, dance the quadrille, adopt Christian names, use your knife and fork correctly, deny your own being and transform yourself into an Englishman. Only then could you be worthy of respect. While Jamaica was granted Independence in 1962, Britannia continues to rule. I wish we would disavow classism" (Kong 2013). Despite the attempt to bring together one people, there were two very different cultures represented in Jamaican music, a tale of two cities, an "ism" schism.

UPTOWN MUSIC

Before 1964 there was no mention at all in the *Daily Gleaner* of ska. The only coverage was advertisements; there were no editorials whatsoever. This is because ska was seen as lowbrow music, music of the downtown, of the streets. Instead of ska, organized independence celebrations included parades with floats and school or military bands. Schools themselves hosted ceremonies with speakers, sacred music, and dancing the quadrille. Public performances for independence included classical music with vocal programs, such as one featuring Jamaican tenor Rudolf Comacho, which was attended by government dignitaries, including Alexander Bustamante. An independence program at the Myrtle Bank Hotel included an array of musical entertainers, including a "late soiree" featuring Lennie Hibbert and His Combo and the Alpha Boys Band, who played "while tea is served" ("Myrtle Bank," 1962, p. 6). The Independence Arts Celebrations, which took place over the entire month of August, featured plenty of dancers and theater, and when it came to music, that too was a "proper" offering. The Festival Orchestra performed "under Carlos Malcolm's baton. Original music for many of the ballets is composed by Carlos Malcolm and Oswald Russell with Malcolm doing the scoring" ("Jamaican Life," 1962, p. 2); the article also listed other credits for lighting, choreography, and guest dancers. There were choral concerts by school groups and men's and women's groups at the State Theatre, as well as plenty of sacred concerts.

Military parades, marches, and band performances took place in towns and villages all over the country. The national anthem was first publicly performed by the Jamaica Military Band at the Lyndhurst Methodist Church Hall just a few weeks before the independence ceremonies. The lyrics were written by Father Hugh Sherlock, and the music was composed by Mapletoft Poulle and his wife, Christine Alison Poulle, although many accounts have Robert Lightbourne involved in the composition as well; the confusion over the true composer is political (Seaga 2012).

Federal Recording Studios engineer Graeme Goodall recalls recording the national anthem. He says that Captain Ted Wade, who was in charge of the Jamaica Military Band, brought the band to the studios in army trucks. "I told him, no problem, we'll record them in the parking lot," said Goodall, because they couldn't all fit in the studio (Goodall, Feb. 8, 2013). As Goodall began running microphones to the lot and then taking sound levels back in the control room, he noticed a problem. "There was traffic outside on Four Shore Road, Marcus Garvey Drive," he says. But Wade radioed the military, who responded by blocking off each end of the road, and the recording went off without a hitch. The band recorded the up-tempo march version for the A side and a slower, vocal version for the B side and Goodall worked all night to press one hundred copies, complete with a label printed with the new Jamaican flag. One record appeared on the desk of each member of parliament the next morning by 9:00 am, and there were copies for RJR and JBC.

Music was important to help Jamaicans bridge their identity from being part of the British Commonwealth to something that was all their own. But the music of the people, the music that was in the clubs and sound systems and studios, was very different from the music played at these celebrations. In 1962, ska was in full swing, much to the dismay of the uptown genteel classes. Even a couple of years later, people writing letters to the editor in the *Daily Gleaner* would call ska "primitive rock with a heavy accent on the off-beat, depending on its monotony for its excitement. The words are indistinct and are usually about animals or parents or children, rather than love and romance. I nickname it the 'Bilious Beat'" (Wilson, 1964, p. 10). Others, like Yvette Bedway (1965, p. 12) of Williamsfield in Manchester, complained that "the ska is raging too much on radio in Jamaica. In the early mornings more services would be welcomed. It gives one a healthier feeling to begin the day with divine service than with the ska tunes." These were not isolated comments. The clubs where ska was played were frequented by either the lower and middle classes or tourists. High-class clubs, the ones up on Crossroads, played a more refined orchestral version of ska by the likes of the Eric Deans Orchestra. Many of these clubs, like the Glass Bucket Club when it was operated by Don Soisson, were once even racially segregated. It is no wonder then that ska did not factor into any of the country's official independence celebrations.

DOWNTOWN MUSIC

Music had always been a part of Jamaican everyday life. The ring game songs, nine-night songs, work songs, and digging songs all had a function. So too did ska music, especially during the days surrounding independence. Ska was born in the late 1950s, and by the time independence was achieved, it was firmly established. But were there not audio records and oral histories of this fact, one might not even know that ska existed around the time of independence, because government musical programs had no representation from ska bands.

Ska was music of the downtown musicians. Patrick Hylton writes:

> Like its predecessors, the Ska was the music of the masses, composed and performed exclusively by poor, black musicians. It was simply unheard of for petty bourgeois musicians like Byron Lee & the Dragonaires, Kes Chin and the Souvenirs and Sonny Bradshaw to play the "repugnant" Ska to their bourgeois audiences. The socio-economic status of a musician determined the type of music he played; the audience to whom he played; and the type of rewards he received. Thus, third-class musicians like Byron Lee were rewarded with fame, money, and prestige, while the greatest musicians Jamaica had ever produced, such as Don Drummond and Ernest Ranglin, were treated with indifference. (1975, p. 27)

But there were plenty of independence celebrations that featured ska music, as advertisements reveal. The Hotel Flamingo hosted Sonny Bradshaw & His Combo for "exciting music for dancing" to "celebrate independence at the poolside terrace" ("Hotel Flamingo" 1962). The Carib Theatre hosted the "Independence Showcase," featuring such ska musicians as The Blues Busters, Byron Lee & the Dragonaires, Keith 'N' Enid, Derrick Morgan; Derrick Harriott, Jimmy Cliff, and Hortense Ellis ("Independence Showcase" 1962). The Deluxe Theater was host to the "Independence Ska-Ta-Rama," with The Skatalites, Derrick Harriott, and Lord Creator; lucky ticket holders even won "free cases of Red Stripe Beer" — quite a juxtaposition to the tea served at the uptown celebrations.

Like everyone else, ska musicians and bands embraced the promise of independence. Independence gave people hope, opportunity, and freedom, especially in the poor and working-class neighborhoods, and ska singers commemorated those feelings in their songs, such as Lord Creator's classic "Independent Jamaica." Lord Creator, a native of Trinidad, reports that Vincent "Randy" Chin approached him to write the song: "It was January, but Chin asked me to make an Independence song for him in tribute to the independent referendum that was approved by the people. I did the song, then I left Jamaica to complete my tour," says Lord Creator, and then when he returned, Chin informed him that the song had been selling faster than "hot bread" (quoted in Mills 1998). Chin asked him to write more songs for him, so Lord Creator followed up with other independence songs: "Welcome Princess Margaret" and "Freedom Song." The lyrics to "Independent Jamaica," a calypso-flavored tune, chronicle the story of securing independence, and it is actually a good account of the events. But the lyrics do more than just tell the tale; they also offer a tone of optimism and hope and foretell the benefits in the future.

Derrick Morgan also wrote a song in commemoration of independence: "In 1962 now, I made this one, when Jamaica was getting independent, I wrote a song called 'Forward March,' getting to the independence, and it was a big sellout. It was a boom. And on the Independence, we on the truck [sound system] going around singing that song 'Forward March'" (1997). This song also has a tone of excitement and optimism and equally acknowledges both parties involved in the process. It is both a narrative and a statement of the buoyant mood of the people during this period. It is patriotic, spiritual, and in direct contrast to the songs in future years that lamented the crime and poverty of the people. This song was a hymn to the nation's vision of the future.

Jimmy Cliff's "Miss Jamaica" embraced the national identity while acknowledging the troubles the country faced. The act of "crowning" is both an act of establishing the prize, independence, and a reference to the British Commonwealth, the Crown, which had been taken back by the Jamaican people and was only theirs to give—they had the power. In the song, Cliff accepts his nation as it is, problems and all, and is proud to call it his own. Al T. Joe's "Rise Jamaica—Independence Time Is Here" is a Fats Domino–style tune, with lyrics assigning aspects of Jamaican independence to each letter of the word "independence," such as nation, democracy, economics, progress, and equality. Joe also references the problems of Jamaica, perhaps British colonial rule, but he asks his people to overcome these problems by moving on, again with a tone of optimism and excitement. Joe White & Chuck offered their "One Nation" in the spirit of independence. The lyrics are also positive and hopeful and stress the unity of one people, both men and women. The words literally ask, as did Derrick Morgan's tune, for the nation to join hands and become one entity.

There was also The Skatalites' "Independence Anniversary Ska," originally named "I Should Have Known Better," a cover of a Beatles tune, which The Skatalites performed in the independence parade in August 1965 on the Cable & Wireless Float. This song had no lyrics, but was nevertheless written in the same spirit of celebration. Jamaica's own music, ska, required no lyrics to express the independence of the new nation. Ska music, like the Jamaican people themselves, was a blend, a collective, of other forms, yet it was original and very distinctly Jamaican. The fact that ska gave rise to rocksteady, reggae, dub, and dancehall in future years also demonstrates how the people's identity as one nation is reflected in the creation of a national music. Sonjah Stanley Naah has written that, "poor people went to the dancehalls. The dance provided physical, ideological, and spiritual shelter for a generation of lower-class Jamaicans, a generation mature enough by the time of independence when the music ska became popular. They asserted a new sense of self, a sense of freedom that was reflected in the beat and tempo of the music and dance" (2006, p. 14).

THE NEW YORK WORLD'S FAIR AND THE PUSH FOR SKA

Ska music first began organically in Kingston as a music of the people, in the schools, the studios, the streets, the dance halls, the sound systems, and the hills. But there was also an orchestrated push to use this music as a way to develop Jamaica's tourist industry, which coincided with the days just after independence was obtained. It came from the same spirit, the wish to establish Jamaica as its own country with its own identity and appeal.

The Skatalites were the undisputed leaders of ska, the most talented group of musicians the island had or has ever seen. Why then would they be passed over for selection to represent Jamaica at the New York World's Fair in 1964, as the country hoped to debut ska to the world, to capitalize on the music that was taking over and giving Jamaica its character? Why would officials choose a band that was inferior to even untrained ears, Byron Lee & the Dragonaires? The answer is simple: Byron Lee was an uptown band that played ska, but not with the soul and vigor of The Skatalites. Even though The Skatalites were more popular, they were downtown musicians known for ganja smoking and all kinds of debauchery. The Skatalites also associated with the Rastafari, a people ostracized and persecuted by the government and establishment. Byron Lee had no dreadlocks, was not dark skinned, and was upper class. As Lloyd Bradley points out, Byron Lee didn't play "ghetto music" (*This Is Reggae Music*, p. 135).

As Kevin O'Brien Chang and Wayne Chen explain, "Despite their legendary reputation today, The Skatalites were not necessarily the most popular band of their time. An RJR poll in February 1965 showed them to be only the fourth most popular band in the country. The Mighty Vikings garnered 2,411 votes; Carlos Malcolm's Afro-Jamaican Rhythms got 2,367. Byron Lee and The Dragonaires got 956; Tommy McCook and The Skatalites 273; The Granville Williams Orchestra 20; the Lennie Hibbert Combo 6" (1998, p. 33). Why the numbers shook out the way they did depended entirely on who was being polled. Because it was an RJR poll, one would assume that those polled were part of the establishment, rather than the "downtown" crowds, as the results also seem to reveal.

Byron Lee was chosen to represent Jamaica, to teach the world to "do the ska," by Edward Seaga, who later went on to become prime minister. But at that time he was Jamaica's minister of culture, a job he took after giving up his previous job of managing Byron Lee & the Dragonaires. As a result, ska, as presented at the World's Fair, was as far from the downtown musicians who created the sound as possible. Not only were the downtown musicians blatantly overlooked in representing Jamaica at the fair, but the World's Fair events at which ska was unveiled were far from the sound system yards. Instead, these events were sophisticated, stylish, and socially exclusive. In U.S. newspaper articles covering the World's Fair, dignitaries and the noble class were photographed "doing the ska" with the Jamaican dancers flown in for the occasion. In one article on May 2, 1964, one such dignitary is depicted kicking up his heels in his suit and tie while seated onlookers smile. "When Arthur Murray takes a dancing lesson, that's news! Here the famed dance instructor catches on fast as he learned the 'Jamaica SKA,' newest dance sensation to hit New York," reads the photo caption, noting that the dancers introduced the craze to the "jet set" during an event at Shepheard's at the Hotel Drake on Park Avenue in Manhattan ("Learning to Dance . . . !," 1964, p. 1).

Cathy White's posh "Personally and Socially" column noted at the end of that month, "Oom . . . ska oom . . ska! Oom . . . ska! That's the sound of the 'up' beat on the bass guitar where the latest dance craze, the Jamaica Ska, gets its name. We headed for Shepheard's and to L'Interdit t'other evening and found Park Avenue gyrating all over the place. Leaving our inhibitions in the 'tent' we joined the fun. Believe me, if you can Twist, you can Ska!" (1964, p. 18). The World's Fair Singer Bowl also played host to a "Jamaica ska party" in August 1964, at which Byron Lee and his twelve-piece orchestra, Millie Small, Jimmy Cliff, and others performed for "youths from an assortment of nations" who "twisted, bounced, wiggled, and shook to the rhythmic beats of the Caribbean dance craze known as the Jamaica Ska" ("Photo Stand Alone," 1964, p. 16).

Even after the World's Fair ended, Seaga continued to send his well-connected musicians to the United States to promote tourism to his country, albeit targeting the proper upper class crowds, the ones who had money and could afford to travel to Jamaica to hear the island's music. Seaga's intention was to market the country, to encourage tourism, and although he could be perplexing at times, supporting the music of the people one minute and bulldozing Back O Wall without notice the next minute, he helped to bridge the gap between uptown and downtown. He helped to bring ska to the world.

Seaga's support of ska was not exactly met with widespread enthusiasm. He had to fight to encourage ska's survival, a testament to his passion for the music. In an editorial for the *Daily Gleaner*, William Strong criticized Seaga for backing ska and said his ears were "bombarded round the clock from every corner of the island with ska music . . . and the sight of a roomful of young people doing ska is more reminiscent of souls in Dante's Inferno than of civilized humans dancing." He criticized Seaga for spending money to promote the island in this way, calling ska gutter level. "It appeals to the lowest instincts," and he accused Seaga of trying to ruin the country with ska (Strong, 1964, p. 10). Fellow politicians wrote open letters to the newspaper, lambasting Seaga for his excessive expenditures promoting ska.

"The Ska and its supporters were subject to the incessant mockery of the petty bourgeoisie, and the music was outlawed by the radio stations" (Hylton, 1975, p. 27). Still, Seaga pursued a deliberate strategy, because he saw that ska was connected to the newly independent Jamaica and the nation's cultural identity. He founded the Jamaica Independence Festival, a showcase of Jamaican arts, which included an all-island ska and mento competition. At the first annual festival, Byron Lee & the Dragonaires performed, of course, and the festival was hosted and funded by the Ministry of Development & Welfare ("Jamaica Festival" 1964). The first festival was held in 1962 to celebrate and coincide with independence. Seaga continued the festival each year after that, and in 1966 he introduced the Popular Song Competition, through which many ska artists, like Toots & the Maytals, gained popularity. Seaga's recording studio, West Indies Records Ltd. (WIRL), produced souvenir records with ska called "I'll Remember Jamaica" from, of course, Byron Lee & the Dragonaires, so tourists could "Take Jamaica Home with you!" (1966) as the advertisements read.

Ska's success in becoming part of Jamaica's national identity surrounding independence was organic, came from the people, and percolated up through the people. Still, having a champion with money to throw behind it in the name of independence, even if the vision was to turn ska into a commodity, helped to bridge the gap between uptown crowds and downtown crowds. Ska music was a source of pride, albeit not for everyone. For those who saw its potential and those who lived with, relished, and performed it, ska was an uplifting music, full of promise. It was a reflection of the promise that independence itself held. It belonged to the people, and it gave the people belonging. Jamaica's many forms of music—classical, choral, folk, ska, rocksteady, dub, dancehall—are all part of one Jamaica, whether overtly promoted as an attraction to the island or simply heard on a radio in the street.

DECLINE OF SKA IN JAMAICA

No single event brought about the decline of ska in Jamaica, nor was there a gradual fading out over years; rather, it was the confluence of a number of events, like a perfect storm. One of the first incidents that caused a waning in ska's popularity was the loss of its greatest musician, genius Don Drummond. Drummond had composed and recorded hundreds of ska songs, so he was a prolific writer, but he was also a profound composer, bringing ska to a new level with his haunting minor chords, complex compositions, and lively, catchy tunes. He made producers a lot of money. But he suffered from schizophrenia and regularly checked himself into Bellevue Mental Hospital, where he received brutal treatment, like electroshock therapy and medications that turned him into a "zombie." He self-medicated, using ganja, eating clay, and drinking strange elixirs from paper bags during recording sessions. His behavior was erratic and was probably acerbated by the lack of success and compensation he should have received for his skill. On January 2, 1965, in the early morning hours, Don Drummond stabbed his girlfriend, Anita Mahfood, to death. Mahfood, whose stage name was Margarita, was a sensational rhumba dancer, a participant in the Wareika Hills, and an outspoken and critical supporter of Rastafarian musicians. She had a challenging relationship with Drummond because he never achieved mental stability. After his arrest, it took a year and a half for Drummond to be declared mentally fit; a short trial was then held. Drummond, represented by P. J. Patterson before he became prime minster, was despondent and unable to speak. He was committed to Bellevue Mental Hospital indefinitely, and there he languished until he died on May 6, 1969, at the young age of thirty-five. Without Don Drummond, the music was never the same.

On April 23, 1966, Haile Selassie visited Jamaica from Ethiopia. Followers by the thousands came by bicycle, car, bus, and foot, swarming the tarmac when his plane arrived in Kingston at Norman Manley International Airport. Throngs of Rastafarians waved Ethiopian flags, blew the abeng, and welcomed their god incarnate. His Imperial Majesty Haile Selassie I, Conquering Lion of the Tribe of Judah, King of Kings (Emperor) of Ethiopia, Elect of God, as his official title styles him, visited sites throughout Jamaica and with the people of Jamaica, including Rastafarian leader Mortimer Planno and Prime Minister Sir Donald Sangster. Selassie was also entreated to attend a performance by Count Ossie and the Mystical Revelation of the Rastafari. The Rastafari had been persecuted and oppressed by the Jamaican establishment for decades. Their camps had been burned, their locks had been humiliatingly cut, and their people had been stabbed and shot. Now, through the presence of Selassie, Rastafarianism was made more acceptable to the government and the establishment. If Rastafarians could be accepted by a foreign dignitary, then perhaps their own country could accept them as well. Rastafarian music—the chanting, the African rhythms, and soon the reggae beat and spiritual content—crept into the nation's musical consciousness, and ska's fervor was not as much a part of that movement anymore.

ROCKSTEADY

Another factor contributing to the decline in ska's popularity was the weather. Kingston in the summer of 1966 experienced a stifling heat wave. It was just too hot to dance with the energy ska demanded. The frenzied, vigorous music literally slowed down to cool off the dancers. A new genre, rocksteady, took over, featuring a more relaxed rhythm, less brass, and more vocals. Vocal duets and crooners took over. There was less and less work for instrumentalists, who began moving to England to try to find work or changing their own styles to accommodate new tastes. Rocksteady only lasted a few years before reggae took over.

One of the crooners given credit for being the first vocalist to introduce this new style is Alton Ellis. In 1966 his single, "Rocksteady," was the first to give a name to the slower sound, but it really wasn't the first rocksteady tune. The lyrics themselves chronicle the fact that rocksteady was already in existence by the time he recorded the song. He was merely storytelling, in a way, about the scenes in the dancehalls and yards. Lyn Taitt has claimed that he was the one who slowed down the beat, and historians give him credit for being the first with his song "Take It Easy," which he recorded with Hopeton Lewis at Federal Recording Studio. "It's very simple. Ska is very fast. Rocksteady is very slow." He says his origins in Trinidad helped him make the new Jamaican sound. "In my country there is fast calypso and slow calypso. In Jamaica only you had fast ska. So I say to myself, 'well, I will slow it down'" (Taitt 2009). The result was rocksteady.

Vocalist Derrick Morgan says that rocksteady was the product of many artists working together and a change in the instruments used, from an upright bass to an electric bass and from a piano to an electric keyboard:

> This musician came down from Trinidad, called himself Lyn Taitt. He have a band called Lyn Taitt and the Jets and they came to Jamaica and this guitarist was Trinidad, but the rest of the players were Jamaican. We were creating a new sound. We're trying to put a bass pattern against the music instead of playing standard string bass on straight,

we use an electric bass now. With ska music we used to use string bass, a tall string bass. But we change it and the first song that made in ska, we use this guy named Herman Sands. He was a pianist. He bring down an electric piano. From there we get the feel of the electric bass and we set a pattern to the bass playing, right? We use an electric bass to set a pattern which is how we get rocksteady now. The pattern of the bass slowed down the music and the piano and the guitar would strum a little slower and the drum would give off one, they call it one drop in Jamaica, so we get a one-drop beat and we call it rocksteady because at this time now in ska music, we used to spin. Hold the girl's hand and let her spin. But in rocksteady, you just rock to the beat. That's why we changed the name now from ska now to rocksteady. You have to re-member, ska music is a foundation. What is ska? It is the guitar and the piano. That is what you call ska. And rocksteady is the same guitar and piano but it is the bass and the drum that changes and make it slower and we call it rocksteady. (Morgan 1997)

In his brilliant book *Solid Foundation*, David Katz has crystallized the difference between ska and rocksteady with words from Leonard Dillon: "Ska is not a matter of speed. Ska is a matter of arrangement. I can play you ska and it's slow; you have slow ska and fast ska, slow rock steady and fast rock steady. The snare drum and the bass drum, the way they drop on your riff, that's the main thing. The bass can be any way, the bass can be slow as ever. Rock steady is the one drop. It's the drum" (2003, p. 67).

The music's origins may have been a bit more organic. In fact, Jamai-can rocksteady, like ska, was probably influenced by music from Ameri-ca, where producers looked for inspiration and trends. American soul music had been gaining popularity in the States for a number of years, but some of the most recognizable songs indicative of the soul movement were recorded in the mid-1960s. Otis Redding's "Try a Little Tenderness" came out in 1966, with the vocalist backed by Booker T. & the M.G.'s, arranged by Isaac Hayes. One year later he recorded "(Sitting On) the Dock of the Bay." During that same year, 1967, another soul star, Aretha Franklin, recorded one of her greatest hits, "Respect," which was origi-nally written and recorded by Redding. In 1968, two more of Franklin's classics, "(You Make Me Feel Like A) Natural Woman" and "Chain of Fools," took over the airwaves as she earned two Grammy Awards. In this era, a great number of other artists made their careers in soul music, especially artists who recorded for Stax Records, such as Eddie Floyd, Wilson Pickett, and Johnnie Taylor, and for Motown, Stevie Wonder, Marvin Gaye, The Temptations, The Supremes, and Gladys Knight & the Pips.

Soul in America evolved into funk as artists like Curtis Mayfield and James Brown brought a new dimension to the sound. In Jamaica, soul blended with ska to produce rocksteady. Derrick Harriott has described the involvement of American soul in Jamaican music, stating that many artists simply covered American soul at first before adopting it into their own repertoire, much in the same way that American R&B came into ska:

> A lot of the new type of American soul music was coming to Jamaica. That's what really eclipsed ska. It was so popular with the people the sound systems were competing for it like they used to with R&B—records were just being imported and exclusives were being guarded just as jealously as they used to be. . . . This new soul music—with the Motown thing as well—was having such an effect in Jamaica, not just records being played on the radio but tours by the artists were always popular. Perhaps inevitably, the Jamaican singers were starting to sing in that style, Derrick Morgan, Dobby Dobson, Joe White . . . Bob Marley and the Wailers were sounding like Curtis Mayfield and the Impressions, Jimmy Cliff sounded like Otis Redding, Ken Boothe sounded like Clarence Carter. Everybody was doing a lot of cover versions. And it was working. And it was slowdown stuff, a lovers' rock kind of thing, and the crowds were going wild. (Bradley, *This Is Reggae Music*, pp. 161–162)

Whereas much of the ska inventory has little in the way of vocals, in the rocksteady years the vocals were the focus of many songs. Both soloists and singing groups made their way in rocksteady, including soloists such as Roy Shirley, Errol Dunkley, and Alton Ellis. But rocksteady was also defined by the vocal groups. In the same vein as The Temptations or The Impressions, there were The Maytals, The Gaylads, The Paragons, The Ethiopians, The Versatiles, The Uniques, The Melodians, The Spanishtonians, The Jamaicans, Johnny & The Attractions, Ike Bennett & The Crystallites, and others. This was not the case in ska. Ska music features instrumentalists, either solo or in a group, but not typically with a group of vocalists.

Also like American soul music, there was plenty of emotion in rocksteady lyrics, and plenty of crying, in songs like "Teardrops Falling," "Cry Tough," "All My Tears," "It's Hard to Confess," "Silent River (Runs Deep)," "The Shadow of Your Smile," "You're Gonna Need Me," and "Do I Worry." These songs were far from the innuendo of calypso, and far from the slackness of dancehall. They were sweet ballads, perfect for couples to fall in love to, perfect to slow down to on a hot night in Jamaica. There were also rocksteady tunes that encouraged aggressive crowds to settle down. The rudeboy tributes in the ska era, like "Rudeboy" by Duke Reid's Group or "Guns Fever" by Baba Brooks Band, became rudeboy songs of warning in the rocksteady era, with tunes like "No Good Rudie" by Justin Hinds & The Dominoes, "Cool Off Rudies" by Derrick Morgan, "A Message to You, Rudy" by Dandy Livingstone, and "Rudie Gets Plenty" by The Spanishtonians.

The unaccommodating weather, the loss of the island's greatest musician, the acceptance of the Rastafari culture and its music, and the emergence of rocksteady sounded a death knell for ska in Jamaica. Ska's heyday spanned 1959 to 1966. But we shouldn't rush to claim "ska is dead," as the joke has been told over the years. Like the people who created this genre, ska was resilient, changing forms many times to blend with those who interpreted it in their own ways. The train to skaville has made many stops, and the next one was England, the land many West Indians immigrated to, bringing ska with them to be heard by new ears, performed by new musicians, and interpreted in new ways.

FIVE

Winter of Discontent

When Margaret Thatcher took office as prime minister of the United Kingdom in May 1979, she came in on the heels of a disastrous previous administration. James Callaghan had brought Britain to a precipice, with widespread union strikes, horrendous inflation, and dreadful unemployment. The nation experienced the worst industrial stoppages due to strikes since 1926. The weather in early 1979 was brutally cold, with terrible blizzards, and gave Britain, both literally and figuratively, a true "Winter of Discontent."

Thatcher's solution to the nation's woes, capitalism, was nurtured by the now Conservative-led government, as neighbors became competitors, each vying for a piece of a dwindling pie. She increased taxes, which hit manufacturing businesses hard, causing many to close their doors and send workers out into the streets. Unemployment rose to its highest level since the 1930s. Competition was now a matter of survival. It was every man for himself in every city, town, and shire in Great Britain. But the tension that led to the evolution of ska in England had begun decades earlier.

IMMIGRATION TO THE UNITED KINGDOM

Britain was devastated by World War II. From September 1939 through May 1945, the United Kingdom was engaged in a conflict that drained its economy of a quarter of its national wealth and utilized 55 percent of its labor force in the war effort. After the war, the nation faced the collateral destruction of its cities and towns; crippling debt; dismal housing opportunities; labor shortages; a weakened currency; and shortages of supplies, which necessitated rationing, never instituted during the war. To help its recovery, Britain opened its doors to immigrants, especially to refugees and the displaced seeking work. Commonwealth citizens, such as those from Jamaica, could enter and stay in the United Kingdom without any restriction, until the implementation of the Commonwealth Immigrants Act in 1962.

On June 22, 1948, 492 men from Jamaica and Trinidad arrived in London after seeing advertisements for labor in their local papers. They embarked on the SS *Empire Windrush* for a small £28 fare, with big hopes for a new life. It was the first of many passages to this new world. "Had they thought England a golden land in a gold age?" asked the *Guardian* newspaper the day following their arrival. "Some had, with their quaint amalgam of American optimism and African innocence" (June 23, 1948). That attitude of superiority over the immigrants, who numbered nearly half a million between that maiden voyage and 1970, met West Indians the minute they stepped off the ship and persisted for decades. Signs outside boarding houses read, "No Dogs, No Blacks, No Irish." If the unfamiliar cold and foggy weather wasn't enough of a slap in the face, surely the blatant racism was.

But the British needed to rebuild, so they recruited Jamaican workers for their medical sector, transportation sector, postal service, and to reconstruct their cities. Britain especially needed hard-working men, the part of the labor force that had been seriously depleted by the war. Musicians who couldn't find work among the dwindling opportunities in Jamaica as ska's success waned moved to the United Kingdom to pursue a musical career abroad or left music behind altogether for other occupations.

It is important to note that immigration to England from Jamaica wasn't necessarily a one-way, permanent move. Rather, immigrants frequently made trips back and forth or sent for members of their families, so they came over in waves. It was a fluctuating exchange, so the spread of culture between the two countries was even more fluid. As Jon Stratton of Curtin University points out, "West Indians often moved to London, and within six months or a year or more later, moved back to the West Indies. Later still, they might move back to England. Culturally, this constant movement of people brought both influences from Jamaica to England and from England to Jamaica" (2010, p. 446). The result was an interchange of communities and their music.

JAMAICAN JAZZ ARTISTS IN THE UNITED KINGDOM

When Jamaicans went to England, they largely settled in London, North Kent, Sheffield, Coventry, Bristol, Birmingham, and Brixton, bringing with them their few belongings in their search for a new life. Among their possessions was their music. Jazz had come to England via Jamaica with the immigration of artists like Joe Harriott, Harold McNair, Wilton Gaynair, and Dizzy Reece, all graduates of the Alpha Boys School Band. Alto-saxophonist Joe Harriott moved to Britain in 1951 and combined the mento and calypso influences of his native Kingston with the jazz of Charlie Parker to create what he termed "abstract" or "free-form" music. Harriott did not go the way of ska and instead pursued other combinations, such as one in the late 1960s with violinist John Mayer, called Indo-jazz fusion, a double quintet consisting of five Indian and five jazz musicians.

Trumpeter Dizzy Reece, whose real name was Alphonso Son Reece, moved to London after leaving Alpha, where he was sent for wandering the streets of Kingston, thereby earning his nickname. He started playing music at age eleven. He became a full-time musician in Kingston in 1947. In 1948, to help him pursue greater opportunities, Reece's mother put him on a ship for England, alone. His proficiency drew the attention of the jazz greats, such as Sonny Rollins and Miles Davis. After issuing his first album in 1959, Reece became the first British jazz star to be signed exclusively by an American record company. He soon moved to New York, where he remained.

Wilton Gaynair settled permanently in 1955 in Germany, where he found ample work, but before that he visited England twice to record for Tempo Records, once in 1959 and again in 1960, and to perform at clubs like the Down Beat Club on Compton Street and the Flamingo Club. This tenor saxophonist went by the nickname Bogey, but to his friends and family he was known as Big Bra Gaynair, because he was the big brother of Bobby Gaynair, fellow Alpharian and saxophonist, who remained in Jamaica to perform with members of The Skatalites as well as many other bands. Bogey played in the same bop style of jazz as Reece and Harriott, as well as other contemporaries. Prior to moving to Europe, Bogey performed regularly with Count Ossie at his camp in the Wareika Hills, so it is no wonder that much of his repertoire is a reminder of the themes echoed in the hills, namely Africa. His nickname, "Big Bra," was also a testament to his time in the hills, and he carried a picture of Haile Selassie with him in his briefcase.

Saxophonist Harold McNair went by the nickname Little G. He, Harriott, and Gaynair were classmates at Alpha, and after McNair left, he toured the Bahamas, playing traditional Caribbean music. When he moved to New York shortly afterward, he took lessons and taught himself to play the flute before moving to London (in 1960), where he found regular work. He even played with Charles Mingus's quartet while Mingus was in London. McNair continued to record and perform, perhaps most notably with Donovan, throughout the mid-1960s.

The British certainly were exposed to Jamaican jazz. Historian and musicologist Herbie Miller has made the connection between Jamaican jazz and ska by describing musicians like The Skatalites as jazz on a ska beat. So the connection for British audiences was not too much of a stretch. They had also already had a taste of Jamaican ska hits from the Blue Beat label and others. In 1964, fellow countryman and connoisseur of all things Jamaican Chris Blackwell produced "My Boy Lollipop" by Millicent Dolly May Small, better known as Millie.

"MY BOY LOLLIPOP"

Millie Small, the bubbly, baby-voiced sprite, traveled to London to record "My Boy Lollipop" for Chris Blackwell. There, as well as back home in Jamaica, the catchy song was an immediate hit, reaching number two on the pop music charts in the United Kingdom. Chris Blackwell had started out selling records in England. He commuted between England and Jamaica to license deals with studios and artists. He grew the Island Records label with deals negotiated with producers such as Vincent Chin, Coxsone Dodd, Duke Reid, Leslie Kong, Lindon O. Pottinger, King Edwards, and Byron Lee. Blackwell saw a market among the West Indian immigrants, but also soon realized that the young white population was starting to develop an affinity for the music. He discovered Millie Small, whom he had heard sing "We'll Meet" with Roy Panton in 1962. "My Boy Lollipop" was the perfect song to appeal to both British and Jamaican audiences because of its sound and familiarity; it had previously been recorded in 1956 by Barbara Gaye, a little-known singer. It was a pop tune that Blackwell mastered to sound even more light and fun when recording the Small version.

Blackwell had already recorded another song with Small, "Don't You Know." He was Small's legal guardian after she moved to England in July 1963. He enrolled her in the Italia Conti Stage School to study dancing and speech, in an attempt to remove her Jamaican patois. He wanted her to appeal to white audiences and not be too exotic, especially because racism was so rampant in England during those years. "Millie's image drew on British colonial fantasies of the exotic Caribbean and she was distinguished from the West Indians who had been settling in England—the racist reaction to whom, in that same year of her success, 1964, provided success for Peter Griffiths, the Conservative candidate for Smethwich in the general election, who used the phrase: 'If you want a nigger for a neighbor, vote liberal or Labour'" (Stratton, p. 452).

The song was also manipulated by Blackwell. He had found the original version by Gaye while shopping for records in New York to sell to the sound system operators in Kingston. He decided the song was perfect for Small, and he brought Ernest Ranglin to England from Jamaica to perform guitar for the track. For the rest of the instrumentalists he used a band called the Five Dimensions, a British blues band. He did this because the song would then have an authentic Jamaican touch as well as an authentic English R&B character, appealing to both audiences. Instead of using the horns found on Jamaican ska tunes, however, Blackwell used a harmonica, typical of American and English R&B, so it would not be too exotic and could speak to the mainstream. He also had the band move the ska beat from the upbeat to the offbeat, which gave it a pop-ska quality, a "galloping ska-style" (Bradley, *This Is Reggae Music*, p. 151). This ska song was sure to be stripped of the downtown ghetto music taint that ska had had among the colonial crowds. "Millie's 'My Boy Lollipop' was received as a novelty song by white Britons," writes Stratton. "This reception was reinforced by Millie's youthful innocence and, ironically, by her blackness. While the West Indians who had come to Britain to work were racialized and excluded from mainstream white society, Millie's blackness formed a part of her exoticization that made her seem attractive and likeable" (2010, pp. 457–458).

Blackwell's creation crossed over between audiences, bringing a Jamaican singer to white audiences in England. The song was a success. It reached number two on the charts on March 14, 1964. A week later, a ska version of the song "Mockingbird Hill" by Magil 5 made it to the top ten on the charts, and nine months later the song "Yeh Yeh" by Georgie Fame and the Blue Flames, which had a ska tone, reached number one. "My Boy Lollipop" launched Small's career, Blackwell's label, and ska as a genre in England. But so too did the success of Desmond Dekker, one of the most influential Jamaican artists in the United Kingdom (and anywhere).

OTHER JAMAICAN ARTISTS IN THE UNITED KINGDOM

Desmond Dekker, born Desmond Adolphus Dacres, had a talent for singing even as a very young child, performing the tunes of artists popular in the United States. After moving to Kingston at age fifteen, he attended Alpha Boys School. Later in life, Dekker began working as a welder apprentice, but after his fellow employees heard his singing, they encouraged him to seek a career in music. Like so many of his contemporaries, he performed at the "Vere Johns Opportunity Hour," and he took time off from work repeatedly to audition at the leading studios of the day. He auditioned for Coxsone Dodd and Duke Reid, but both turned him down. However, Leslie Kong saw Dekker's immeasurable talent, and after a couple of auditions in front of Derrick Morgan and Jimmy Cliff, accompanied by pianist Theophilus Beckford of "Easy Snappin'" fame, Kong signed him to the Beverley's label in 1961 and he sang backup for Derrick Morgan for two years with his brother, George Dekker, before taking off on his own.

In 1967, rudeboy culture was commemorated in Dekker's huge hit "007 (Shanty Town)," which reached number one on Jamaican charts, as well as number fifteen in the United Kingdom. The tune even became a hit in the United States, and it was also featured in the movie *The Harder They Come*. Dekker wrote the song about the violence among Jamaican youth in the late 1960s. For British youths who glamorized such stylish culture, the song sealed Dekker's position as an icon. He continued to celebrate rudeboy culture in many of his tunes. The concept of the rude boy spoke loudly to British white youths. "White and black working-class youth in decaying urban centers in Britain (and to a lesser extent in the United States) adopted the Rude Boy idiom as a tool of protest amid a climate of disintegration and decline in the fortunes of working-class families. Rude culture, ska classics, and the latest reggae dubs provided an interracial youth culture with nascent renegade identities and served as a crucial backdrop to the wave of intense riots that rocked British cities in the mid-1970s" (Heathcott, 2003, p. 197).

In 1968, Dekker won the Jamaica Festival song contest with "Intensified," and in the same year he released perhaps his most popular song, "Israelites," which solidified his position as one of the greatest Jamaican artists of all time. The song was such a huge hit in Jamaica that Commercial Entertainment, a management company, brought him to the United Kingdom to tour. When he inked a deal for Trojan Records in 1970, Dekker made the move to England permanent.

Listening to this song once will reveal the appeal that Dekker had to his audiences, but in the United Kingdom his style and charisma also made him a star. White youths emulated his fashions, including wearing short pants. When Dekker came to Britain in 1967, he was given a stylish suit by his recording company, Creole. He cut six inches off the bottoms of the suit pants to create a new style. The kids responded to this style by rolling up the bottoms of their pants, a trend that became part of subculture dress code.

Laurel Aitken, the godfather of ska, was born in Cuba in 1927 as Lorenzo Aitken. He moved to Jamaica when he was eleven years old. His career, like many others, was launched by the "Vere Johns Opportunity Hour," and he found success in 1958 when Chris Blackwell produced his first song, the hit "Boogie in My Bones," on the A side, with "Little Sheila" on the B side. But Aitken saw more opportunity to make money in England, so in 1960 he left Jamaica for greener pastures in Brixton. He found that his records had been pirated in the United Kingdom by Emil Shallit and his Melodisc label. Aitken made no money from their sales. He confronted Shallit about the crime, and the two men negotiated a compromise, striking a deal for a new label called Blue Beat, dedicated solely to Jamaican ska. Aitken released a number of hits on this label and others over the many years of his career, such as "Hey Bartender," "Jenny Jenny," "Boogie in My Bones," "Sally Brown," "Scandal in a Brixton Market," "Rudi Got Married," and "Skinhead."

Rico Rodriguez, born in Kingston in 1934, attended Alpha Boys School like so many others. He was sent there by his mother after he had been hit by a car and injured while skipping school and getting into trouble at the loading docks. He learned to play trombone under the tutelage of fellow trombonist Don Drummond, who was his mentor, and Reuben Delgado, bandmaster at Alpha. Rico performed in studios around Kingston and had some success with songs like "Easy Snappin'," with Theo Beckford. He was a session performer for Clue J & the Bluesblasters and for Duke Reid's Group. He also recorded with a number of other Jamaican producers, including Randy's. He regularly visited the Wareika Hills, where he honed his musical skills and his spirituality. He became a devout Rastafarian and lived at the camp until he moved to the United Kingdom in 1962. There he continued to record and joined forces with Georgie Fame, a British R&B artist. Rico performed for a number of British producers, labels, and artists.

Other Jamaican artists moved to England over the years, seeking the fortune and fame that their native land never gave them. "In Jamaica, artists were simply paid for the recording that they made and their producer then earned a profit by sales of the single. If the artists knew that there was a significant market in England then they would have asked for more money to record. Consequently, the producers were keeping quiet about their sales in England" (Stratton, 2010, p. 443). So the Jamaican artists moved. They made England their home, and although racism was a fact of life they dealt with daily, they also experienced a warm embrace as their music received a new audience and a new interpretation.

BLUE BEAT

Those who lived among the new citizens and their music, the white youths in Brixton, Coventry, and Birmingham, called their new infusion of Jamaica ska what they thought it was, Jamaican blues or blue beat. In 1960, a British ska label was launched by Siggy Jackson, a record producer who heard the Jamaican sound at a party. The Blue Beat label was a subsidiary of Melodisc, Emil Shallit's label. The label promoted artists such as Laurel Aitken, Prince Buster, Derrick Morgan, and Owen Gray to the British market. Blue Beat even brought Count Ossie and Duke Reid to London from Kingston to play shows in Brixton and Lewisham. By the end of 1963, Blue Beat was at the height of its popularity, fueled by Jamaican independence the year before. The label stayed in business from 1960 to 1967; during that period it released four hundred singles and twelve albums by Jamaican artists. According to Laurel Aitken, producers at this label, not unlike their Jamaican counterparts, kept the profits and royalties for themselves, and the artists saw little profit from their art. There is a persistent rumor that Shallit could be seen during his scouting trips to Kingston with a red suitcase in hand, stuffed with cash and records, with the words "Danger: High Explosives" written on its sides. Despite the corruption, Blue Beat and Island Records were the two top ska labels in England, importing ska music for those who craved the sound, both the West Indians who longed for the music of home and the white youths who heard the music at neighborhood bars played by Jamaican deejays.

JAMAICAN DEEJAYS

When West Indians moved to England, they were met with a dirty, dark, foggy climate, unlike Jamaica's, and blatant segregation. There was no place for black people to go and they were not allowed into clubs, so deejays like Duke Vin and Count Suckle turned to hosting parties in the flats of friends and in basements, where they played their Jamaican collections of records. They could also send for music from Kingston, and at these house parties, guests could commiserate with their fellow West Indians and hear news from back home.

Duke Vin, born Vincent George Forbes, moved to London in 1954. He learned his way around a sound system by working for Tom "the Great" Sebastian in Kingston. With a fantastic collection of Jamaican music, Duke Vin built the first sound system in England, the Tickler, in 1955, when he couldn't find any dances like the ones he had experienced in Kingston. He set up his first system at Ladbroke Grove in London and bought his records from a West London record shop owner named Daddy Peckings, who carried vinyl from Sir Coxsone Dodd's Studio One label. Duke Vin continued deejaying for the rest of his life, spinning at the Marquee Club, the Flamingo, Brixton Town Hall, the Ram Jam Club, the Roaring Twenties, and Stoke Newington Hall. In true Jamaican fashion, he engaged in sound system clashes with fellow deejays, one of whom was Count Suckle.

Count Suckle, whose real name is Wilbert Augustus Campbell, moved to England in the same year (1954) and in the same manner as Duke Vin, as a stowaway on a ship. When the captain discovered Count Suckle, the ship was too far along on its journey to turn back. Count Suckle's sound system, named after himself, was used at parties all over London before he secured a residency at the Roaring Twenties on the West End of the city. Count Suckle played his records between sets by a live band that played to a white and black crowd. They came together for the music, R& B and ska, which was unlike anything else played in London at the time. Count Suckle opened his own club in 1962, called the Q Club, in Paddington, and he founded a record label, Q Records, an imprint of Trojan Records.

Other Jamaican deejays in England during the 1950s and 1960s were The Coleman Brothers (Arnold and Cecil), Ossie Holt, Count Shelley, Sir

Dick, Count Myrie, Duke Brown, and Count C. They played to unite their people, performing everywhere from garages to ballrooms. They played records at clubs like the Ram Jam in Brixton or the 007 in Dalston. They played plenty of music imported from Jamaica, which they secured on their trips home, as well as records from their own collections, which they had brought with them when they immigrated. But they also found music in Britain when more and more British labels sprang up to cater to West Indians and white youths. Not only did Blue Beat and Island Records record Jamaican artists, but others were established, like Plani-tone (Orbitone in later years), Trojan Records, and Pama Records.

Trojan Records was established in 1967 as an imprint of Island Records. It only released about a dozen of Duke Reid's productions. The label was named after Reid's sound system in Jamaica; the van in which he carried his equipment was made from an imported Trojan kit. In 1968, businessman Lee Gopthal took over the label after his other label, B&C (Beat & Commercial), merged with Island Records. The label released more of Reid's productions, along with work by Lee Perry, Bunny Lee, Clancy Eccles, and some British producers.

Pama Records, a competitor of Trojan, was established by three broth-ers from Jamaica, Carl, Jeff, and Harry Palmer, in 1967. It released vinyl from such Jamaican producers as Clancy Eccles, Bunny Lee, and Lee "Scratch" Perry, along with artists Alton Ellis, Derrick Morgan (with his classic "Moon Hop"), and Max Romeo, whose "Wet Dream" sold over a quarter million copies and was perhaps Pama's most popular hit.

WHITE YOUTH

British bands like The Beatles and The Rolling Stones entered the world's consciousness during the 1960s. The music industry in England was en-gaged in producing more bands that would appeal to the screaming throngs of girls, bands such as Herman's Hermits, The Animals, and Gerry and the Pacemakers. But as the years went by, white youths in England longed for something with a little more edge to reflect the grow-ing discontent they were feeling with their own lot in life. In the 1970s, they turned away from arena rockers like T. Rex, Led Zeppelin, Jethro Tull, Thin Lizzy, Queen, and Pink Floyd. As that decade waned, so did the heavy sounds of endless rock anthems. No more "Scaramouch," no more flute-playing minstrels, no more Black Country rock. White youths had other things on their minds, like getting away from the stress of unemployment, labor strikes, and inflation. Life was hard. They had no prospects for a good future. Just like their Jamaican counterparts two to three decades earlier, struggling British youths found sanctuary in the optimistic sounds of ska.

Reggae and ska were a medium of expression, a talking drum, a talking rhythm. And young whites had much to say. Instead of American R& B, now living side by side with its West Indian neighbors, white British youths were influenced by the sounds of the Caribbean. It was part spirit of rebellion, part association with the message.

SUBCULTURES

Like the rude boys of Jamaica, England also had subcultures that identified with the music, and the music with them. Dress code was important as a group distinction, and styles segued from Jamaica into the wardrobes of white culture in England, especially among the working class.

One such group was the mods. Mods were aligned with the working class, but with attention to being hip and dandy. They wore short, cropped hairstyles, and girls frequently had their hair cut short on top with bangs, but with long fringes around the face and the back. Mod boys wore sophisticated suits, crewneck or V-neck sweaters, or button-down collared shirts and thin neckties, whereas mod girls wore button-down, white-collared shirts and miniskirts. The mods drove scooters, which not only made them able to move quickly from club to club, but also brought the group a sense of solidarity. They wore military parkas to protect their stylish clothes from the elements while riding. Mod culture was all about the style, an aspect that would find its way into ska. Dressing exquisitely enabled the mobile mod to transition among all facets of his or her life, from day to nightclub. The Specials' song "Nite Klub" chronicled the night-in, night-out ritual of attending club after club that became the mods' lifestyle, even though they worked menial jobs during the day, if they worked at all, in order to purchase threads more glamorous than those worn by their bosses. It was a way the mods had control over their domain in unforgiving times.

"The Rude Boys' white counterparts, the Mods, who were investigating these new and exciting inner-city clubs, soon took to the snappy new West Indian dress style and adapted some of the elements into their wardrobes," writes Laurence Cane Honeysett of the cross-pollination between rudeboy and mod culture. "Almost as quickly, they started to fill their record boxes with the records they heard played in the clubs. The obligatory pork-pie hat was closely followed by the equally mandatory Prince Buster blue-beat record into the annals of Mod must-haves, along with a cut of Jimmy Smith's grooving Hammond B3 and a Small Faces album" (Honeysett and de Koningh, 2003, p. 114). The success of much Jamaican music during this time can be credited to the mods—music such as Prince Buster's "Al Capone," which reached number eighteen on the British charts in early 1967.

The skinhead culture in England was built out of the more aggressive mod culture of the mid-1960s and in response to the hippie culture and populations of preppy students that had flourished in the preceding years. Skinhead culture first emerged in 1969, perhaps in the East End of London. The pressure felt by the working class during the "Winter of Discontent" in 1979 gave them a reason to solidify, to re-create the working-class communities they saw dwindling. Their mothers and fathers before them, the working class, were to be respected, and they formed families of their own, skinhead mobs or a patch, based on their neighborhoods or areas where they lived. Groups, such as the Quinton Mob and the Smethwick Mob, had a strong sense of identity, a value that would become part of ska culture, but they fought with other skinhead groups, as well as with other subculture groups, such as hippies or rockers, over control of their territory. At times they experienced camaraderie at large gatherings, like soccer games, but mostly the skinhead groups clashed with one another. This was the skinhead way of seizing power over their communities, which had been chiseled away for years.

Skinhead dress, aspects of which would be adopted by future ska fans and band members, was characterized by rolled-up jeans, combat boots, thin braces (called suspenders in the United States), and a Ben Sherman or similar button-down style shirt. Hair was either completely shaven or worn short. Girls wore miniskirts, tights, combat boots, oxfords, or loafers, and a permanent-press shirt, with or without braces. Hair styles worn by girl skins, or lady birds, were short on top and fringed and long around the edges, varying in length. Skinhead dress may have been a response to styles of the era, but there is also evidence suggesting that some of the dress code may have involved a transition from the rudeboy look in Jamaica. In Jamaica, clothing and a sharp look were important to rude boys who wanted to attract attention. They wore suits made of shiny fabric that glistened in the nightclub lights, and a pork pie hat was common. This hat featured a narrow brim, and Laurel Aitken was almost never without one.

Punks also found ska music's energetic tempo enticing and they, skinheads, and mods frequented the pubs where the Jamaican artists and deejays performed in West Indian neighborhoods and towns. Boots became taller; anger became angrier. Violence between groups—punks and skins, punks and hippies, punks and teds—was rampant, as each clamored to defend its identity in a symbolic fight for survival. "At first sight the punks seemed unlikely reggae fans. With their dyed spikey hair, ripped T-shirts and day-glo bondage trousers, they looked completely different from the black British reggae fans. What's more, the Rasta creed of 'peace and love' didn't seem to fit in at all with the punk rockers' violent image. But though the frantic, moody beat, there were obvious similarities between the two types of music" (Hebdige, 1987, p. 96). The similarities were in the message. Jamaican music talked of Babylon and the decline of the establishment, and so too did punk music talk about the establishment in Britain and the problems of living under it. Rastafarians were ostracized and persecuted by the Jamaican society, as punks were shunned and rejected by proper British society. Even Bob Marley sang of the similarities in his "Punky Reggae Party." Parties at which subcultures like punks congregated at friends' homes featured a blend of the two forms of music: an hour of punk, an hour of reggae. The punk music would energize dancers, and the reggae would give them a chance to mellow and regenerate. It was an unlikely combination, but acted as yin and a yang. For those who found the two forms of music too much at odds, the solution was clear—ska, through which they returned to the roots of the reggae to find a tempo more akin to punk, a similar energy, a similar message. Even though ska's message was frequently communicated with horns, the anger, the persecution, the sadness, and the poverty were still felt.

Another subculture group that formed as a result of punk's popularity was the Oi! movement. Whereas punk music could sometimes just be performance related, and members were frequently art school graduates or dropouts, Oi! bands prided themselves on being working class, and that is why they formed as an offshoot. Fans of Oi!, named for Cockney slang for "hello," thought that punk had become too commercial. Oi! bands like Sham 69, The Business, The Cockney Rejects, Angelic Upstarts, The 4-Skins, Combat 84, Blitz, and The Blood combined the raw energy and anger of punk with soccer-like chants from the backup vocalists. They sang about police brutality, injustice, murder and rape, jailbreaks, police states, unemployment and poverty, stealing and looting, and the politics that created a desperate situation for the working class. They were part of a populist movement, a movement of the people. Sham 69 was so much of the people that it brought audience members up on the stage and even backstage after the show, where all doors were open.

Many other subcultures shared similar experiences and interests. The teddy boys in the 1950s took Edwardian-style clothing and flaunted it in a rebellious manner. They wore long jackets and tweed vests and slicked back their hair. In the 1970s, they made a comeback when Vivienne Westwood and Malcolm McLaren adopted that style of clothing for their Let It Rock shop on London's King's Road. Suedeheads, so named because of their close-shaven heads, were similar to skinheads but were an offshoot of that group. They dressed fancy, in brogues (Oxford dress shoes), loafers, or basketweave Norwegians rather than in skinhead boots. They also wore crombies, three-quarter-length dress coats, and sometimes suits. Another group, called smoothies, smooths, smooth mods, or peacock mods, were kinder, gentler mods, less violent and fancier, distinguished from hard mods or gang mods. There were splinter groups throughout these subcultures as cliques of individuals formed with their own nuances, distinguished by patches or paisley scarves or variations on these themes.

BROTHERHOOD AND UNITY

Subcultures like mods, skinheads, and punks boldly wore their identities on their sleeves, sometimes literally, to express their pride and exert their power in the only way they could. Music also became part of the subcultures' identities. Not surprisingly, the music each group adopted became a mélange of the influences around them, and the West Indian culture became part of this blend. Jamaican imports combined with the music popular among the subcultures, both musically and in the topics about which they sang. Soon, attendance at clubs featured more white youths than West Indians. Record labels began producing music that catered to the sounds the white youths craved, releasing titles such as Symarip's "Skinhead Moonstomp" and a large number of tunes from Judge Dread and Laurel Aitken. White artists like Bob Dylan, The Rolling Stones, Paul Simon, and The Beatles started to adopt the reggae rhythm. But there was a call for something more, something different.

The result was the second generation of ska, a sound different from its Jamaican ancestor, although it still employed the syncopated beat, the horns, and the lively tempo. The music, once again, was an outlet for people to enjoy dancing as a means of escape, but it was much more than a simple Saturday night sound track. This ska, just like its father, acknowledged the state of affairs in the world and described the people's struggles, the rampant unemployment and racism and crime, and it offered the hope of brotherhood and unity.

SIX

British Ska in a Fractured Nation

Jamaican music and culture had been simmering in the United Kingdom for a decade and a half before ska finally broke into the British consciousness. While Millie Small's "My Boy Lollipop" turned a whole new audience on to ska, namely white British youths, ska then took root as numerous transplanted Jamaican artists played and spun their tunes in British clubs. Throughout the 1970s, Jamaican music was largely underground in the Brixton neighborhoods where West Indian immigrants lived, although it periodically surfaced.

In the late 1970s, however, Jamaican music in Britain took a very different turn. White working-class youths seized on ska, blended it with other musical genres, and spit it back out as a new sound, so unrecognizable to Jamaican natives that they claimed it wasn't the same animal at all. It was unpalatable to their authentic tastes. British ska didn't evolve the music, said many, and in fact some claimed it took the music further away from its roots in jazz and calypso. British musicians interpreted ska through a different lens, of punk and pop music. They also saw ska through the lens of their white brothers and the Jamaicans they idolized, and through the lens of the politics of nationalism, socialism, and racism.

POLITICS AND RACISM

To understand why ska blended with punk and pop music in Britain as it did, we must first look at the cultural and political climate that created the medium for the music, because like its Jamaican predecessor, ska music was more than a set of notes and rhythms—it was a messenger for the people's voice. Leading up to the late 1970s, unemployment was rife, especially in the working-class neighborhoods where West Indian immigrants and white youths lived side by side. Although most mods and other subculture groups respected West Indian immigrants, there were some who did not share this feeling of brotherly love. Some racist skinheads, driven by the high unemployment rate during the late 1970s, pointed accusingly at West Indian immigrants, whom they blamed for taking jobs away from the British (a situation akin to the current U.S. immigration conflicts). Riots took place in West Indian neighborhoods and Britain's major cities as white youths became enraged over their desperate situation. Black people were bullied, even though unemployment was highest among their population. Even Margaret Thatcher, before she became prime minister, blamed violence on immigration in a 1978 television broadcast: "People are rather afraid that this country might be rather swamped by people of a different culture" (1978 TV interview).

Nationalist movements took hold in Britain during the late 1960s and 1970s, including two that grew powerful through their membership, organized recruiting techniques, and violence. The British Movement used swastikas and photos of Adolf Hitler on its propaganda, advocating the use of violence in its anti-immigration efforts. Its members entered politics and ran on right-wing, anti-immigration platforms. The National Front called for the phased deportation of all nonwhite immigrants and demanded a ban on further nonwhite immigration into Britain, claiming that it stood for "white family values."

Conversely, other white youths embraced the policies of the Labour Party, working-class ethics, and socialist ideologies advocating that opportunity should be equally available for all, regardless of skin color. They aimed their frustration, not at the West Indian immigrants, but at the source of the strife, the British government, which set the policies that created the unemployment. They blamed the establishment for monopolizing the palatial wealth and biscuits and crumpets, which were savored by few and shared with none. It was from this culture that the punk ethic was born.

ANARCHY IN THE U.K.

In the mid-1970s, a number of punk bands began popping up all over Britain with a raucous sound and DIY (do it yourself) principles. They did not want stuffy old codgers calling the shots on how they led their lives, nor did they want huge corporate record labels telling them how to play their music (although they would eventually enter into tumultuous deals with big labels and write songs about it). They didn't have to have their guitars in tune, because that would be following the rules. They were discordant. They shocked, they offended, they were filthy and vulgar. They were angry, and they fought against anything they saw as an injustice or establishment. Bands like The Stranglers, The Damned, the

Sex Pistols, and The Clash, who performed at punk clubs like the Roxy, led the charge. Punk was more than just music—it was a movement.

Punk songs did more than just criticize the existing undesirable situation. Lyrics also envisioned a new society, one with more freedom and prospects. The Sex Pistols wailed about having no future and dreamed of an economy that would give them opportunity instead of war. The Damned sang about a society without police harassment, no laws, and no money to buy guns, while The Stranglers sang of being driven into the sewer to live and of wealthy, beautiful people. The Clash shouted about class warfare, race, wealth and power, unemployment, riots, police, and the failures of capitalism. They all conveyed a strong message beneath it all: stand up and fight!

Punk was a subculture embraced largely by white youths. There were virtually no black members of punk groups, except for a few such as Don Letts, Poly Styrene, and Ranking Roger, because punk music spoke to white youths about those aspects of British culture they found themselves in. Punk music was familiar to white youths in the United Kingdom, performed by white British artists, about white British themes, with sounds akin to the rock music that preceded it. Black music in Britain was palatable to whites if it was familiar, with an R&B or pop spine, instead of being strange and exotic like roots reggae. When white youths got tired of being angry, but still needed a group that understood and embraced them, they turned to music with a much different sound, but the same message: ska.

At the same time that punk was developing, a branch emerged that was not quite punk but had similar musical experimentation, attitude, and energy. New wave musicians in the United Kingdom, like Elvis Costello, Ian Dury, Ultravox, and Gary Numan, performed music with choppy guitars, fast electronic tempos, and synthesizer flourishes. New wave, despite its departure from traditional R&B formulas, was still pop music, albeit with a geeky feel. It did not carry the political and cultural messages of punk, and in fact its song lyrics could be without meaning at all, about cars or car trouble or wanting to be a machine, or about a futuristic world.

BRITISH SKA AND WHITE IDENTITY

Sharing much of the same audience and the same message, it was a natural development for punk music to blend with the Jamaican ska in neighborhoods of the unemployed and marginalized. Punk and ska had already started to merge when The Clash incorporated Jamaican music into their repertoire, using Jamaican beats, both reggae and ska, in their music; referencing Jamaican culture; and covering Jamaican songs. Joe Strummer of The Clash has said that this decision was a conscious one, and he even met with members of the Sex Pistols to discuss the use of reggae in their music, and although the Sex Pistols did not like the idea, The Clash gave it their own interpretation.

It was Jerry Dammers, however, who is credited with bringing ska, punk, and a bit of pop and new wave music together. Without Dammers, ska in England would have been little more than an underground ebb and flow of social activity. Born in India in 1954, Dammers came to be a part of the British experience when his family moved to the country when he was just two years old and then settled in Coventry when he was ten. He dabbled in a number of subculture groups—mods, hippies, and skinheads—in a working-class city built on the auto industry. He was a somewhat troubled youth, getting into fights and into trouble at school. At a young age he was attracted to the sounds of ska, which he heard in his neighborhood, as well as American R&B and Motown. He started his own band and began experimenting with a fusion of reggae and punk that led him to form The Coventry Automatics, a band whose name was soon changed to The Specials.

Lynval Golding of The Specials remembers how the music came together. "We had songs where part of the songs were reggae, then they'd go into a rock section, then perhaps back into reggae. And it would throw people off. . . . So we sat down and looked at the whole thing and put a definite beat in it all the way through, sort of blended it together" (quoted in Rambali, 1980, p. 32).

Dammers intentionally chose some of the members of his band to make a statement to the nationalistic and racist groups that were gaining strength in England. He says he thought that as a way to "get through to these people," the racist skinheads who rioted during soccer games and at concerts, using ska instead of reggae would communicate better. Dammers included two West Indian members in his band, Jamaicans Lynval Golding and Neville Staple. At first they were reluctant to play ska because they associated it with their parents and thought it was oldies music. In fact, Barbadian Silverton Hutchinson, who was the band's first drummer, left the band when the decision was made to turn from reggae to ska. Dammers also brought in Rico Rodriguez, a Jamaican trombonist and graduate of Alpha Boys School who performed in Kingston's studios, giving authenticity to the music while attempting to incorporate a broader audience. Dammers saw ska as a medium for his message. Adding vocalist Terry Hall to the lineup brought in an element of new wave, because Hall's style of deadpan, monotone singing appealed to the new sound. To solidify the connection to the Jamaican music that the subcultures craved, The Specials covered Jamaican original songs through their own interpretation of punk and pop, as well as creating their own tunes, with Horace Panter, Roddy "Radiation" Byers, and John Bradbury.

Serious about the political platform that ska provided, Jerry Dammers embraced the DIY attitude of punk, coming up with his own identity for the band and establishing his own label, 2Tone, an imprint of Chrysalis. Other ska bands either stayed on the label for the duration of their run or got their starts on the 2Tone label before they also adopted the DIY attitude and created their own labels. To further his message, Dammers incorporated black and white in the marketing for 2Tone. He used a checkerboard motif and drew upon his art school background to design the band's logo and mascot, Walt Jabsco, a character adapted from Peter Tosh's photo on the cover of The Wailers album. These designs, these themes, helped to solidify an identity for white youth audiences.

The message of identity and unity is perhaps made most apparent through The Specials' use of stage invasions. Stage invasions were part of the performance each time The Specials played, because Jerry Dammers felt that there should be no separation, no hierarchy, between performer and audience. "It's important to keep on the same level as the people who buy your records," Dammers once said. The band allowed members of the audience to join them up on the stage, which was fun for the audience, and a raucous good time for the band at first, until lighting rigs and staging started to collapse. When Dammers would yell "Nobody is Special!" during these invasions, he literally meant that everyone was equal, everyone was in the same predicament, everyone was part of the same Britain. It was a statement against the bourgeoisie.

To further solidify the group identity, the ska revival in Britain featured a unique ska dance, the skank. According to Timothy White in *Catch a Fire*, the skank originated in Rastafari culture. "Dreads would sit on their haunches in tight circles, passing the chillum pipe, a clay hookah with an 'unskanked' (unbent, hence the name of the dance step) six-inch tube" (White, 1983, p. 225). Because the dancers bent themselves with the rhythm, it was called the skank.

A variety of dance moves appeared during the Jamaican era. Historian Verena Reckord writes, "Like all popular Jamaican dance forms, the ska came with its own set of movements; a kind of charade to music in which the dancers brought into play things like domestic activity (washing clothes, bathing), recreation (horse racing, cricket), actually anything that appealed to the ska dancer at the moment. Some really fancy and furious 'foot works' came out of the ska period" (1982, p. 73).

The skank during the British era was similar in many ways to its Jamaican predecessor, but it was also different because it combined elements of other musical genres and the frustrations of the dancers. Instead of merely swinging the arms back and forth, crossing them at times as they did in the 1960s in Jamaica, the British form of the skank incorporated balled-up fists, perhaps in response to the anger of post-punk times. The British skank also incorporated more vertical bounce, probably integrating the pogo, the punk dance that may have been invented by Sid Vicious himself, whereas the Jamaican version often left the feet completely stationary.

Ska music has always been about dancing and audience participation, and the effect of hundreds of young people, bobbing and jumping to the frenetic tempos of the music, was contagious. To listen to The Specials live, followed by The Selecter, followed by The Beat, all on one bill at one venue, was to be swept up in the moment, to be delivered from the discords of society through the harmony of sound, dance, and intoxicating communion. Often the dancing on stage was silly, even nutty, as Madness called their own special brand of humor and dance. The subject matter of songs, if not serious commentary on politics or society, could be the complete opposite—silly and nonsensical, to bring levity to a depressed culture.

Outside of the concert hall, ska music continued to provide an identity for white youth by establishing a subculture all its own. They called themselves rude boys or rude girls, reminiscent of the Jamaican gangsters who had roamed the streets of Kingston two decades earlier. They adopted some of the elements of other subcultures they associated with, such as riding scooters like the mods or shaving their heads and wearing braces and boots like the skinheads, because there was overlap among many of the subculture groups. But members of the ska revival subculture had a distinctive look. It was sharp, reminiscent of the Jamaican experience of dressing well. They wore the pork pie hat, a chapeau similar to a fedora but flat on the top, with a narrow brim. They wore oxford shoes, polished and neat, and tonic suits purchased from thrift shops. They also wore sunglasses, even at night. The effect this had was to visibly distinguish the members of the ska subculture, the rude boys and rude girls, from other groups and draw its members together by having them look alike. Consolidated together, they were powerful over their powerless situation. They were a common voice, and they *were* special. Terry Hall once claimed that the clothes were almost as important as the music.

BRITISH SKA BANDS

Other bands either serendipitously joined the ska revival or jumped on the bandwagon. They all had an eye toward sending a message on race and unity. The Selecter featured a mixed race lineup led by enigmatic and brilliant vocalist Pauline Black. Black was influenced by the Jamaican vocalists she heard on her friends' turntables, the artists who were popular in East London where she grew up, despite the fact that her neighborhood was not ethnically or racially diverse. She was influenced by the baby-like voice of Millie Small and her tune "My Boy Lollipop," as well as by Desmond Dekker and his popular song "Israelites," and by The Pioneers and Toots & the Maytals. She began singing at local clubs around Coventry and grew through her affiliations with other musicians, eventually leading her to the other members of The Selecter. Black found bass player Charley Anderson, drummer "H," Charles Bembridge, and keyboardist Desmond Brown. After Lynval Golding from The Specials turned up at a rehearsal, he suggested they meet with Neol Davies, and The Selecter was formed. Davies not only helped to write much of the band's material with Black, but also to negotiate the band's involvement in the 2Tone contract with its band, The Specials, and Chrysalis. All fourteen members of the two bands were to have an equal share in the label.

The English Beat (called The Beat prior to the discovery of a U.S. band with the same name) emerged from the soot and grey skies of Birmingham, a largely industrial city known as the "workshop of the world." Not only was the environment heavy in Birmingham, but so too was the music up to that point, as bands like Black Sabbath and artists like Robert Plant and John Bonham of Led Zepplin from Stourbridge, just outside of Birmingham, laid the foundation for Black Country rock. To express their love for music and music writing, vocalist Dave Wakeling and school chum Andy Cox combined with David Steele while living in the Isle of Wight, then returned to Birmingham to add Everett Morton, who was born in St. Kitts, and vocalist and toaster Ranking Roger. Elder Jamaican Lionel Martin, known as Saxa, rounded out the lineup, on saxophone.

The Beat, like The Selecter and The Specials, had a racially mixed lineup. Their song lyrics were about love and unity, and they also frequently took a political stand against the Thatcher-led government and the jobless conditions they and their fans faced. Their songs could also feature slower ska tempos and pop rhythms, and they were greatly influenced by the members' growing selection of African records as well as African and Chinese instruments. The connection to Jamaican ska, however, was strong. One of their most popular albums is titled *Wha'ppen?*, which is a Jamaican term that Ranking Roger used to say to the band to ask them "What's going on?," very akin to a phrase used by Cluet Johnson in Jamaica in the 1960s, "Wha'up Skavoovie?," from which "ska" may have been coined.

The all-female lineup of The Bodysnatchers featured the provocative and soulful Rhoda Dakar on vocals. Formed in 1979 by Nicky Summers, The Bodysnatchers' first concert was in West London, opening for The Nips, Shane MacGowan's band before The Pogues. After they performed at Debbie Harry's birthday party, Jerry Dammers signed The Bodysnatchers to the 2Tone label, and in the summer of 1980 they toured with The Specials and the Go-Go's, another all-female band. Although they lasted less than two years and recorded no albums, The Bodysnatchers were influential in the ska movement. Like Pauline Black, they showed that women could have a role in ska music. The female perspective in ska is perhaps portrayed best in the song "The Boiler," which deals with the issue of rape and low self-esteem and was based on a real account. The song was recorded by Rhoda Dakar and Nicky Summers with The Special AKA after The Bodysnatchers disbanded.

British ska bands across the board collaborated with original Jamaican musicians, on tour, in the studio, and by covering songs like "A Message to You, Rudy," "Carry Go Bring Come," "Train to Skaville," "Rough Rider," "Monkey Man," "Too Hot," and "You're Wondering Now." They honored the roots of the music and literally brought it to a new generation of admirers by spawning a genre, but they also sent audiences a message about race—that black and white could cooperate to produce something magnificent.

Members of Madness and Bad Manners were all white, and although they may not have been making an overt statement on race in their musical makeup and their lyrics, they did fulfill another important function of the ska revival, a paradoxically compatible one: to provide a sense of white identity. All ska revival bands shared in this function, even though their lineups and messages may have been about race, because white identity wasn't racist, it was a force against the policies of the British government, the administration, the establishment that resulted in their collective struggle. It was empowering to be together and satisfying to see others in a similar plight. It was a way to be nostalgic, together, for a time when no one was treated as a second-class citizen, black or white.

For many members of Madness, coming together in a band to play was simply a way to stay out of trouble in the harsh economic environment. It was a way to keep out of jail, especially for Lee "Kix" Thompson and some of his other childhood friends, who founded the band from the boys' club they attended after school. Their style was a blend of music with absurdity and performance, part Jamaican ska, part Frank Zappa. First called the North London Invaders, Madness was fronted by the suave and silly Graham McPherson, known as Suggs. Paying homage to their Jamaican roots, specifically Prince Buster, they recorded "The Prince" in 1979 on the 2Tone label before leaving to go to Stiff Records and record their classic album, *One Step Beyond*, another nod to Prince Buster.

Bad Manners, equally silly with an equally Caucasian lineup, albeit with a message of unity, was formed by Douglas Trendle, better known as Buster Bloodvessel, and his schoolmates from Woodberry Down Comprehensive School. Influenced by Jamaican ska, Bad Manners was also influenced by Louis Jordan, Louie Prima, Chuck Berry, Otis Redding, Fats Domino, and the Bonzo Dog Doo Dah Band. The band released their first album, *Ska 'N' B*, in 1980, but they gained more success, and perhaps notoriety, from their wild live performances on such shows as *Top of the Pops*. Singing while eating a pickle and cheese sandwich, dressing up as Henry VIII or a can-can dancer while riding around on a bike, and even mooning the television camera in Italy while the pope was watching were all part of the appeal.

It is important to note the significance of the names of the British ska bands. These names often paid homage to the Jamaican era of ska. The Specials, for example, took their name from the concept of the special, a one-off recording that sound system operators like Coxsone Dodd and Duke Reid made to compete with each other at the sound system dances. The Selecter took their name to acknowledge the sound system selecter, the one who chose the records to play at the dances, the songs that would cause such frenzy that they drew the largest crowd to their yard. The Beat requires no explanation, except that it was recognition of the importance of rhythm in the music, and it was a name akin to The Clash, which Ranking Roger acknowledges as part of their aim in taking the moniker. Madness, like their namesake song, not only reflected the band's nutty character, but paid homage to Prince Buster, whose song they covered.

RACISM AND BRITISH SKA

White identity had the effect of binding together youth culture in a common Britishness, but it also had the opposite effect for those who were already inclined to racism or had been members of racist subcultures. Despite attempts by Dammers and other ska revival bands to oppose racism through their lineups, the subject matter of their songs, and their marketing, one look at the audience at a typical concert during these years exposed a blatant reality. The audiences were almost exclusively white. Even though there were massive ties to Jamaica, ska music in Britain did not appeal to West Indians. By the time the late 1970s and early 1980s rolled around, the West Indian immigrants were on to something new—not old ska, but roots reggae, which was too exotic and *other* to be appreciated by white working-class youths, who were nostalgic for the Britain they knew before unemployment. Ska's social experiment did not have the intended effect of bringing together black and white in unity.

This reality became even more apparent with the rampant racism of the British Movement and National Front, whose members attended ska concerts to riot and recruit. They fed on the frustrations and energy of the white unemployed youths with their white supremacist rhetoric. In the 1970s, the British Movement and National Front had grown greatly. Playing on the desperation of white unemployed youths, these racist groups pointed the finger at immigrants rather than administration and government policy. Members of these political parties ran on platforms banning nonwhite immigration. They took to the streets to demonstrate and march and were met with protests, and violent clashes ensued. Members of the National Front and British Movement attended Oi! concerts and instigated violence. As a result, many Oi! bands became involved in anti-racist organizations, including The Business, who named one of their tours "Oi Against Racism and Political Extremism . . . But Still Against the System." Members of the British Movement and National Front also attended ska concerts, strangely enough. Racist skinheads frequently sieg heiled in the crowd. They called the band The Specials plus two, a derogatory reference to the two nonwhite members. They also threw coins with force at the black members of the bands and spit at them. Lynval Golding, guitarist for The Specials, was subjected to racist attacks on two occasions, one of which nearly killed him. After a show at Shades Club in Coventry City Centre on January 7, 1982, a group of white racist criminals attacked Golding, slashing his face and throat so that he needed twenty-eight stitches. He nearly died because the knife came dreadfully close to his jugular vein. His eyesight was permanently damaged. Even though The Specials and other British ska bands sang about love and unity, racists continued to use violence at shows. During the last British tour, Jerry Dammers and Terry Hall of The Specials were fined and spent the night in jail for "inciting violence," even though they urged the crowd to stop throwing cans at each other and onto the stage and to stop fighting with each other. "We did everything that we could to stop the fighting. Everything possible," said Dammers. "We told everyone that unless the fighting stopped, we'd leave the stage and it did work but . . . the bouncers were fighting too against a group of kids. . . . Our efforts did stop the violence so I don't know why we got arrested" (Millar, 1981, p. 32). As a result of these outbreaks of violence, concert venues and promoters grew reluctant to book ska bands. The message of love and unity either fell on deaf ears or was not heard at all.

ROCK AGAINST RACISM

Concert organizers sought to combat the growing nationalistic and racist movements in England by founding their own anti-Nazi groups, such as the Anti-Nazi League and Rock Against Racism (RAR). Although RAR had been an idea in organizers Red Saunders and Roger Huddle's minds for some time, they decided to act in August 1976. They formed RAR in response to an incident in which Eric Clapton, drunk onstage, asked if there were any foreigners in the audience and said that if there were, this was the reason everyone should support Enoch Powell, a right-wing member of parliament who was anti-immigration. Clapton told the crowd that England was becoming "overcrowded" and a "black colony," and he said that people should "get the foreigners out, get the wogs out, get the coons out," then repeatedly shouted the National Front slogan "Keep Britain White." Such rhetoric fostered racial hatred, so RAR organizers held concerts and staged marches with the slogan "Love Music Hate Racism." Anytime a National Front rally was held, more RAR and Anti-Nazi League supporters turned out to oppose and discredit their efforts. RAR concerts featured a variety of bands to appeal to all races and musical tastes, including punk and ska. The Specials performed many times for RAR concerts in their early days as the Coventry Automatics, and they headlined the final RAR concert in 1981 in Leeds.

"Rock Against Racism remains the most single-minded and, in that single-mindedness, successful force for political change in the history of music," writes Dave Thompson, author of *Wheels Out of Gear: 2Tone, The Specials, and a World in Flame.* He quotes Gene October, vocalist of the punk band Chelsea:

> Before the Rock Against Racism thing really got going, if you were white, there were parts of town you simply didn't go into, because the blacks would kick the shit out of you, not because they were racist, but because you might be. The black kids wanted to mix and later, after punk happened and Rock Against Racism got going, they could. You'd walk past a bunch of Rastas and they'd be fine, 'How you going, mate?' You'd get black kids at punk show, punk kids at reggae shows. That simply couldn't have happened a year earlier. That's how much Rock Against Racism changed things. (Thompson, 2004, p. 35)

GHOST TOWN

In early 1981, The Specials met in a small studio in Leamington to record a song that best captured the zeitgeist of the ska revival. "Ghost Town," a song with an eerie, haunting, discordant sound whose words echoed the violence on the streets, was serendipitously and coincidentally released at the same time that massive rioting took place across the country. The song's words, "Can't go on no more, the people getting angry," prophetically paralleled police randomly stopping and searching people in Operation Swamp, so named because of Thatcher's comments about people being "afraid that this country might be rather swamped by people of a different culture." Most of the 943 people who were searched in six days were black. As a result, rioting broke out in Brixton, Coventry, and literally dozens of other towns and neighborhoods. Hundreds of people were arrested, and people were murdered in racist attacks. "Ghost Town" was ska music's version of the Sex Pistols' "God Save the Queen" about no future. It was more than a warning—it was a declaration. The song reached number one on the charts. "Music didn't cause the riots, of course," says TV Smith, vocalist for the Adverts, in Thompson's book. "But songs like 'Ghost Town' helped make people aware that there really was something wrong with the country, and when you realize something is wrong you want to do something about it" (Thompson, 2004, p. 181). Lynval Golding opined, "'It's terrible when you have a song like that and you see that, gradually, it's all coming true. . . . It's a bit frightening when you predict something's gonna happen, it's always horrible when you actually see it's coming true'" (Du Noyer, 1981, p. 19).

In many ways, "Ghost Town" marked the end of the ska revival, because it threw in the towel. It was the last single the original lineup of The Specials recorded together, as members split up to try their hands at other bands, projects, and genres, and The Specials were the seminal ska revival band. But "Ghost Town" also threw in the towel because the aim of the ska revival, the aim of Jerry Dammers, had been achieved: the West Indian immigrants were no longer accepting "no dogs, no blacks" lying down. Through the revolution and rioting, they were standing up and demanding to be recognized as equal. They were no longer West Indian immigrants—they were British citizens.

WHY SKA IN THE UNITED KINGDOM WANED

Although ska music in Britain may have continued for a few years after "Ghost Town," the message had been heard. Ska music was enormously popular in England from 1979 until about 1982. The Specials' first release, "Gangsters," immediately hit the top 10; the next 2Tone band, Madness, hit the top 20 with their first release, "The Prince"; the third release for 2Tone, "On My Radio" by The Selecter, hit the top 10; The Beat's first release on 2Tone, "Tears of a Clown," hit number six on the charts; and the hits kept coming.

With such quick and massive popularity, why did ska music begin to disappear from the charts around 1983 or 1984? Some of the bands, like The Specials, broke up because of internal factors. Two years after forming, The Specials dissolved their original lineup into other incarnations. A combination of influences took their toll on the band members, who were really just boys, experiencing too much too young. They were teenagers who thought the fame would never end. Even though external politics were important to the members of the band, and they drew together to deal with these issues, they simply were too young and too inexperienced to deal with the internal politics of seven bandmates, each one autonomous and each clamoring for a piece of the pie that had become very bountiful without much notice. Dammers and Roddy Radiation literally fought in the studio over the musical direction of the band. Similar quarrels occurred between members of other bands, like The Beat and The Selecter. Touring for eight weeks at a time while fighting and arguing among themselves grew tiresome.

When ska bands crossed the pond to tour the United States, they found little response from the arena crowds, who sat in their seats and did not understand the music's very British message. Bands like Def Leppard, REO Speedwagon, and Journey were big in the States; at their concerts, masses of people could light their lighters to ballads about love and women and sway together, not listen to silly songs about British unemployment and racism. An article in British rag *New Musical Express* in 1980 poked fun at The Specials' first tour of the states, calling, "Oklahoma City, the real hick cowboy heartland of middle America, where the Specials play to a rabid crowd who holler for *rack and rowl* when what they mean is Foghat or ZZ Top. . . . [S]even hundred residents of the Bible-belt no-liquor state of Oklahoma, who—unlike their cosmopolitan New York cousins—had no idea what to expect let alone how to respond when they got it, who have never heard of ska, blue-beat hats and tonic suits, whose fellow citizens think a crop is a 'goddamn faggot military-style hair-cut'" (quoted in Rambali, 1981, p. 30).

Another article detailing The Specials' first tour of the United States touched on the difference in the politics the band represented, which was not represented in American society. Garry Bushell commented:

> They don't muck about the Yanks. These buildings go all the way up like the architect was getting paid by the cubic foot although exactly what good they do anyone escapes me for the moment. They're almost frighteningly blank, their sparkling glass exteriors, mirroring what some observers would doubtless describe as the faceless fascist nature of the upper echelons of American society, and they must have cost a bomb, yet we're literally minutes away from real disgusting poverty, the mostly non-caucasian slums that breed hookers and junkies and vicious crime. (1980, p. 31)

In a nutshell, British ska was British. It didn't translate.

In addition, the musical tastes of listeners in England started to change. It was the end of an era. The Selecter's Pauline Black points out: "You have to remember that 2Tone was this brief blip at the end of the punk movement lasting only a couple of years before the New Romantics took over, when bands like Yazoo (known in the U.S. as Yaz) and Duran Duran suddenly became popular. Our music became passé and the whole movement just died for a few years, completely. The music audience in Britain is very fickle" (2007, interview with author).

Lineups started changing, and continuity diminished. Labels like Chrysalis and Sire, which spent big bucks to market ska bands in the United States, lost money and soon dropped their contracts or changed terms. 2Tone bands started to leave the label to pursue their own interests, and some of them left the ska genre behind entirely. By January 1981, only two of the five bands signed to 2Tone remained, The Specials and Rico. The Selecter, The Bodysnatchers, and The Swinging Cats had left. "I don't really know the personal reasons behind the splits," Dammers has said. The members of The Selecter gave as their reason that they needed "more attention and more help" from a label. Robbi Millar offers another reason for the split: "Possibly, 2Tone would have been a stronger corporation if it had been less of an incestuous operation. Most of the bands involved were, after all, friends or colleagues of the Specials and, looking back over a period of time, events might have been less sticky had some total outsiders been brought into focus" (1981, p. 33).

When the political and social climate changed, so did the music. Political and social situations grew worse, more serious. Racism reached a breaking point, and ska music could no longer be jovial and nostalgic in the face of rampant rioting. To say, "can't we all just get along" against the backdrop of such intense anger, frustration, and death was trite. So how then did ska music cross the pond?

2TONE COVERS: AN APPENDIX

Following is a list of cover songs or interpretations of Jamaican originals released on the 2Tone label. Since the days of 2Tone, the tradition of covering or being inspired by the Jamaican ska greats has produced thousands of songs.

The Specials:

> "Gangsters," inspired by "Al Capone" by Prince Buster
> "A Message to You Rudy" by Dandy Livingstone
> "Too Much Too Young," inspired by "Birth Control" by Lloyd Charmers
> "Guns of Navarone" by The Skatalites
> "Longshot Kick De Bucket" by The Pioneers
> "Liquidator" by Harry J Allstars
> "Skinhead Moonstomp" by Symarip
> "Rude Boys Outa Jail," inspired by "Rude Boy Gone a Jail" by Desmond
> Baker & The Clarendonians
> "Too Hot" by Prince Buster
> "Monkey Man" by Toots & The Maytals
> "Stupid Marriage," inspired by "Judge Dread" by Prince Buster
> "You're Wondering Now" by Andy and Joey and later The Skatalites
> "Enjoy Yourself" by Prince Buster

Madness:

> "The Prince," inspired by "Earthquake" by Prince Buster
> "Madness" by Prince Buster
> "One Step Beyond" by Prince Buster

The Beat:

> "Ranking Full Stop," inspired by "Pussy Price" by Laurel Aitken

The Selecter:

"Everyday (Time Hard)" by The Pioneers
"My Boy Lollipop," inspired by Barbie Gaye and later Millie Small
"Carry Go Bring Come" by Justin Hinds
"Murder" by Leon & Owen & Drumbago All Stars

The Bodysnatchers:

"(People Get Ready) Let's Do Rocksteady" by Dandy Livingstone
"Too Experienced" by Winston Francis
"007" by Desmond Dekker

Rico:

"Oh Carolina" by The Folkes Brothers
"Easy Snappin'" by Theophilus Beckford
"Do the Reload," inspired by "Green Island" by Don Drummond
"Don't Stay Out Late" by Lord Creator
"That Man Is Forward," inspired by "Joker" by The Duke Reid Group

*Source: "Under the Covers." 2-tone.info/articles/covers2.html (accessed March 28, 2013)

SEVEN

East Side Beat

How then did ska cross the big pond to the United States, when American masses had already sampled the goods and decided to pass? Like its ancestral versions, the ska that had begun as a man-in-the-street form of music rooted in the people of Jamaica, that continued as a mixture of black roots, white youth, and the blue collar in England, now progressed again as a do-it-yourself underground movement in the United States, slowly simmering anew with potential and promise.

Much of ska's trajectory up to this point could be credited to immigrants spreading the sound with recorded music carried by hand from one country to another. With ska being as much live music as recorded music, it is no wonder that the live performances of 2Tone bands in the United States, as well as immigration, contributed once again to the development of the genre.

THE TOASTERS AND MOON SKA RECORDS

Although thousands of teens would be influenced by 2Tone and British ska throughout the 1980s and 1990s, it was really the relentless passion of one man that was responsible for bringing ska to America, launching an East Coast movement. Just as West Indian immigrants took their music to England in the 1950s and 1960s, a British immigrant, Robert "Bucket" Hingley, brought his music to the States. Hingley moved to New York during the height of the 2Tone ska era in England. Having been in a couple of bands in the United Kingdom (I-Witness, The Klingons), Hingley had an affinity for music that was popular in his native country, including punk, ska, and reggae. After Hingley saw the English Beat perform live at Roseland in New York City on their American tour, he was stunned by the nearly empty stadium and thought the music deserved attention and held promise. "The place was empty. So at that point I was on a mission from God," Hingley once said (Nickson, 1997, p. 33). He formed a band consisting of his fellow Forbidden Planet comic book store coworkers. The band, first called Not Bob Marley and then called The Toasters, performed their first gig at CBGB, the famous Manhattan club known for launching punk rock in the United States with the likes of The Ramones, Patti Smith, The Cramps, Talking Heads, and dozens of others. By 1983, The Toasters had a residency at the club.

Early on, The Toasters changed their sound dramatically by adding two vocalists to Bucket's lead. Sean "Cavo" Dinsmore and Lionel "Nene" Bernard were known as the Unity 2. They not only added energy and showmanship to The Toasters' performances, but they also added musical toasting, chatting, which brought an authentic ska feel to their repertoire. But the hip-hop genre was emerging in the United States, and Unity 2 definitely had the hip-hop sound, so they decided to leave The Toasters and venture off on their own to pursue hip-hop instead of ska. Still, Unity 2 serve as an example of the link between toasting and hip-hop.

The Toasters had a tie to punk rock in the United Kingdom, especially since ska music was shaped by the punk sound and ethic in England, but The Toasters, by performing shows on the same bill as punk bands at a punk club for punk audiences, had a tie to punk in New York. The Toasters also shared their rehearsal space with punk bands: Bad Brains, Murphy's Law, Agnostic Front, and others. Hingley had also performed in punk bands in his early years.

The punk DIY ethic guided Hingley's creation of his own ska label, Moon Ska Records, in the tradition of 2Tone. He named the label to pay homage to another renowned label, Sun Records. Hingley says he started the label because he could not find anyone to release The Toasters' music, which was not a vendible sound at the time. Marketers could not figure out if this new sound, ska, was white music or black music, so they didn't know where to put it. Venues like CBGB and bands like the Ramones have only grown legendary over the years—back in the early 1980s, performing at a club with bands of this stature was not an indication of having made it. On the contrary, The Toasters and ska music were certainly underground and would remain so for many years. Establishing an independent label, like Moon Ska Records, may very well have been the only way to disseminate the music at this time.

Commercial radio, MTV, and the music press were still largely segregated at this time between "white" music and "black" music. Ska music was not easily classified and did not easily fit into these artificially created and imposed categories. It wasn't until 1982 that MTV aired the first black artists in a studio segment, and that was the group Musical Youth with "Pass the Dutchie," a bowdlerization of the Mighty Diamonds' reggae song about smoking ganja. The video was directed by Don Letts, British reggae and punk deejay, so it is surprising that this video did not open up more doors for not only black artists, but also ska and reggae music, in the commercial mainstream, especially since it was a big hit. Instead, bands that played ska, like the 2Tone bands or the emerging U.S. bands, were lumped by the market into the new wave category, where the lines between musical subgenres and white and black music were blurred or ignored.

Moon Ska Records was officially founded in 1983 and released The Toasters' first album, an EP called *Recriminations*, in 1985. It was the first independently released U.S. ska record to be nationally distributed. Soon other bands with similar musical tastes began to crop up and appear on the Moon Ska label. The New York Citizens (previously Legal Gender), The Boilers, Urban Blight, Beat Brigade, and The Second Step all had releases on the Moon Ska label. In 1986, Moon Ska marketed the burgeoning bands in a move that both allowed ska in the United States to thrive and ultimately killed it. *New York Beat: Hit & Run*, an appropriately named album, was a compilation of many of the ska bands and related genres on the Moon Ska label, along with a few others like the A-Kings, City Beat, Cryin' Out Loud, The Daybreakers, Floorkiss, The Press, and The Scene. The compilation was in a sense a sampler. It allowed listeners to hear the sounds of a variety of ska bands and pursue further releases from individual ska bands if they wanted. This was done in an age before CDs and of course the Internet, so the vinyl compilation was an innovative way to market the Moon Ska offerings and give audiences a decent helping of ska. It was an American buffet of ska, a snapshot of the New York City ska scene in the mid-1980s, and it demonstrated how the collective New York ska sound had evolved from 2Tone. It also spread the sound throughout the country and inspired fans to create their own ska bands. The release of this compilation was accompanied by a concert. The show, called Two Tone Two, featured five bands on one bill at Danceteria, another endeavor that would introduce many sounds to many people all at once. The first compilation to debut the sounds from all over the country on the Moon label was *Ska Face* in 1988.

It is important to draw attention to another aspect of the compilation that helped to visually provide an authentic American feel to ska, the cover art as comic book illustration. Hingley was manager of Forbidden Planet, a comic book store, and he employed comic book artist Bob Fingerman to illustrate the cover of a number of Moon Ska Records compilations, as well as Toasters' covers. Fingerman designed the covers of the *New York Beat: Hit & Run*, *Skaface*, and *Spawn of Skarmageddeon* compilations as well as The Toasters' first EP, *New York Beat*, and *Skaboom!* His illustrations, at the dawn of ska in America, made it less British and more American, like sticking a hot dog in one hand and a baseball bat in the other.

Moon Ska distributed records from Hingley's various Manhattan apartments in the 1980s and then from his basement in Verona, New

Jersey, in the first half of the 1990s. When not on tour, he filled the mail orders from fans himself. Steve Shafer (2012), who did promotions and marketing for Moon Ska throughout the 1990s, remembers:

> Everything was done, especially in the beginning, with a handshake. It wasn't until deep into things that we had to have contracts or lawyers or licensing agreements. That became kind of a drag. We were just partners in it and we weren't going to dick each other over. It was that philosophy and ethos on which the label was run. Bucket really wanted everything to be collaborative. It was a mentality that was non-competitive, that we can all raise each other up and make this work. Bucket's vision for the label and the scene was about helping each other. I don't think he ever really quite got the credit for that.

In 1995, more than a decade after the founding of the label, Moon Ska finally grew large enough to open up a storefront in addition to its distribution center located in Verona, New Jersey. The store was small, but teenagers could come in and browse for ska, punk, and even Oi!, a subgenre of punk made popular in the United Kingdom by The Business and in the States by The Press. It was inevitable that the faster tempos of punk and Oi! and their more aggressive and experimental feel would seep into ska's repertoire, as would the antifascist, socialist, antiracist ethic. The store was first located at 150 East 2nd Street in Alphabet City. "It was a little sketchy," says Shafer of the neighborhood back in the day. "There was a methadone clinic down the block, and it was tiny, the size of a barbershop. There was room for 10 people to come in with the stock and staff. We took our first tentative steps into a retail wing of the business. This was pre-internet and people would come by and talk to staff. A lot of people didn't even have email yet and so a lot of it was word of mouth" (2012). It was the first time a ska label had a place of commerce, and Moon Ska stocked ska from all labels, not only its own, as well as imports. The store moved to 84 East 10th Street when it outgrew the digs.

EARLY NEW YORK CITY BANDS

It is important to take a look at some of the early bands in New York City, without which The Toasters and Moon Ska Records would have been relegated to a single band distributed by their own label, which wasn't unheard of. Instead, New York City had its own ska scene, bolstered by the punk movement, because ska bands and punk bands frequently appeared on the same bills. The bands who played ska during these early years were a galvanized force that brought ska to the country.

Urban Blight first formed in the 1970s when its members were all twelve-year-old students in Manhattan playing rock 'n' roll music. They went on to open for such national groups as UB40, Duran Duran, the Red Hot Chili Peppers, and Cyndi Lauper, and in the early years the Beastie

Boys opened for them. Vocalist Keene Carse also played the drums at the front of the stage. Carse grew up in the music industry; his father was a roadie for bands and he frequently got to go backstage at big shows as a child. Members of Urban Blight were mostly influenced by classic rock until they heard "Stand Down Margaret" by The Beat, which changed their sound forever. In 1982, the band packed up and went to London to perform and listen to other bands. Like a bird bringing a seed across the ocean to sprout a new species, Urban Blight returned to New York City, where they frequently performed at CBGB, then a melting pot of punk and ska. They spread their sound to other cities on the East Coast, such as Baltimore and Washington, D.C. It was a classic example of "cross-polli-nation."

The A-Kings were a three-piece band who produced only a demo tape, so they truly lived up to the idea that ska must be experienced to be appreciated. Influenced by The Beat's *I Just Can't Stop It* album, the band featured no horns, only drums, lead guitar, and bass guitar, but they still performed in the ska genre. They went on to perform with Fishbone and The Untouchables and appeared on the Moon Ska Records *Hit & Run* compilation with a song called "7259." This number was assigned to one of the members of the band in high school after their student records were computerized, so it was an identification number that the band used to play into the 007 spy theme.

The Boilers were first known as The Unseen and were influenced more by roots reggae than ska. They too appeared on the *Hit & Run* compilation and performed at the same venues as the others, but perhaps the most notable legacy of The Boilers is their trombonist, Jeff Baker, who is also known as King Django. Baker went on to record with and perform in a number of heavy-hitting ska bands, such as Skinnerbox, Stubborn All-Stars, and Murphy's Law, and as a solo artist.

The Second Step featured a female vocalist, Remi Sammy, who, like Pauline Black of The Selecter, brought moxy to the stage. Formed in the same way that so many other ska bands have formed, as a group of friends in high school, The Second Step quickly became part of the fabric of New York ska by performing alongside others. They toured incessant-ly, doing over fifteen hundred shows during their career, a demonstra-tion of the power of live ska music and the tenacity required to survive in the genre.

Beat Brigade formed through another method characteristic of New York ska, advertisements in the *Village Voice* calling for auditions. They were influenced by British ska, The Clash, and The Police, as well as by the sound of other New York ska bands who performed at the same venues where they played: the AZ Club, CBGB, and the Knitting Factory. Bassist Frank Usamanont (2009) recalls the early days: "I really felt it was so unique and ultra cool! When we had our first show with the Toasters, The Second Step, The Boilers, A-Kings etc. . . . You would see these kids

in the suits and girls in the plaid, checkered skirts, pork pie hats everywhere! I mean really, scooters would line up outside CBGB's and
Blanches Bar on Avenue A! It was a sight to see! You felt a part of it, you
feel you are part of the scene. It felt great!"

The New York Citizens were led by vocalist Robert Tierney, who
started a band called Legal Gender, which had been on a Moon Ska
Records single. They, like so many others, were influenced by British ska,
and they soon changed their name to the New York Citizens. Their songs
"Sticky Situation" and "National Front" dealt with issues of racism and
fascism, and others tackled South African apartheid, Reaganomics,
homelessness, and other issues.

Ska during this era was largely a live experience. With Moon Ska
Records being one of the only labels that would pay any attention, and
any money, to these bands, recordings during the early 1980s in New
York were either compilations, a new concept, or demo tapes roughly
recorded by the bands themselves, in a rehearsal space or a live venue. It
was a time, not unlike the live era of Jamaican music, prestudio years,
that reinforced the philosophy that ska is a live experience more than a
recorded genre. "You could go and have a great time at a New York
Citizens' show, but you couldn't take the great time home with you except in the spaces of your mind. Hold those memories tight. This world
will never be the same, but I'm okay with that," said Robert Tierney,
frontman for The New York Citizens (quoted in Usamanont 2009) .

AUDIENCE

For fans, the Moon Ska store was a place to exercise their decision to
support independents instead of big chains of the day, like Tower
Records or Coconuts, and the compilations and releases were cheaper at
Moon Ska. An album typically cost only $10. The store was also some-
thing perhaps even more important: a place to commiserate and to share
like interests with fellow comrades. It was a place for kids to go to have a
common identity, an escape from either the tribulations of the gritty city
or the mundane world of suburbia.

A handful of venues booked ska bands in its underground days in
New York. CBGB, the Wetlands, The Cooler, Coney Island High, Danceteria, the Mudd Club, SNAFU, and New Music Café all booked shows,
which were essentially packages of five or six ska bands, on a Friday or
Saturday night. The age of audience members ranged from fifteen to fifty
and comprised fans of punk, 2Tone, and even hippies, who enjoyed the
opportunity to dance at a live show instead of sitting in a vacuous arena
with a lighter in hand listening to droning ballads. This was the era
before hip-hop, before hardcore, during a time of charting artists like

Huey Lewis & the News, Bruce Springsteen, Survivor, Phil Collins, and Tina Turner.

But the live experience was the real appeal of 1980s New York ska, as it was of British ska and Jamaican ska, although perhaps even more so. One reason is that a live show sounded better than the recorded version. The early 1980s saw the birth of the digital era, and electronic instruments made their debut in music of all genres, including early East Coast ska. The DX-7, Yamaha's first stand-alone digital synthesizer, was introduced in 1983 and found its way into ska music, as did attempts at electronic sampling, MIDI technology, and the drum machine. Mixing these emerging (stress on the word emerging!) technologies with the DIY mentality of the era resulted in bad production quality and a sound that in many cases does not stand the test of time. But the live experience was different and could not be reproduced on a recording. An electronic keyboard or synthesizer may have made an appearance on stage, but a drum machine or MIDI technology with wires running hither and yon did not make it onto the tour bus. The live experience was something completely different than the studio album, so fans were more likely to come to a New York ska show, not just for a good time, seeing half a dozen bands on a bill for a few bucks, but because the music was the real deal. It was raw energy, and it sounded good.

The drinking age in New York during the early to mid-1980s was only eighteen, so clubs that booked ska bands typically attracted a young crowd, who then continued drinking afterward at a bar on Avenue A in the East Village called Blanche's. Fans were tight-knit and dressed in styles similar to those of their English counterparts. They had seen the pork pie hats, Fred Perry shirts, oxford shoes, and suspenders worn during the 2Tone tours of New York. But the style this time around was less about brotherhood and more about emulation (and in the late 1980s and early 1990s, one of the few places in New York City to find Dr. Martens shoes and boots and Ben Sherman and Fred Perry clothes was 99X, located just upstairs from the Moon storefront). Clothing styles and dancing styles were seen as synonymous with the ska sound, so skanking and pogoing, created in the United Kingdom, continued in the United States. But ska in the United States attracted different subcultures too, or those who identified with no subculture at all, so a variety of dances and clothing styles could also be on display at live shows. Concerts were a place to be together in a common culture, with a common interest, in an era before cell phones and texting, before e-mail, before any sort of social media or the Internet. Ska shows were a place for sharing a beer and company.

ZINES AND IMAGERY

For those who could not make it to the east side of Manhattan to go to the Moon Ska storefront or were not old enough or lived too far away to travel to New York City to see a ska show, another medium was critical to spreading the word on the world of ska—the zine. The ska zine began as a catalog. Moon Ska Records mailed its *Skazette* to anyone on the mailing list. It told fans about new releases on the label along with artist information and tales of the scene. Shafer (2012), who produced the *Skazette*, recalls: "In the early 90s we had a single page newsletter that I put together on my Mac and I Xeroxed it and sent it to our list, or to mail orders. It was very organic, trying to get that out there. I did that for a couple of years and then we published it on newsprint later."

Shafer says that the idea for communicating through a zine came from Britain, and Moon Ska quickly adopted it. "The only way I would find out about ska in the late '80s was through zines. George Marshall had *Zoot!* and it was fantastic. It was more focused on the British and European scene that flared back up in the late 80s with The Potato 5, The Deltones, The Trojans, and Unicorn Records was huge, so *Zoot!* covered all of that. It had reviews, interviews, and ads and it was one of the few ways to find out about anything in ska, so they were really vital. The zines were really key to ska," says Shafer (2012). When new ska labels established themselves in future years, they followed suit. Stubborn Records, founded in 1992, sent out its catalog/zine *Black and White*; Jump Up! Records, established in 1993, produced *Everything Off-Beat*. And fans had their own zines devoted to ska, like *The Lean CuiZine*, *Ska-doodle*, *Skank*, *Kill Every Racist Bastard*, *Dino's Skaradise Zine*, *Molly Ringworm*, *Ska'd for Life*, and *Ska-tastrophe*, among hundreds of others, with articles, music reviews, trivia, and plenty of novel illustrations.

In an era of social media, blogs have taken the place of the printed zine. But in the 1980s, ska zines were coveted material. Fans were able to keep up with their favorite bands through the zine. Anyone could make and print a zine with a few markers and a copy machine and spread their thoughts and opinions about the latest and greatest bands. Band members were always willing to give a backstage interview to a teenager with a microcassette recorder, knowing the fanzine was a medium for promoting their group. For fans, the zine was a lifeline. By the mid-1990s, there were several hundred fanzines devoted to ska in the States. Illustrations, in the tradition of Walt Jabsco, graced the pages of ska fanzines, depicting rude boys, rude girls, scooters, and a new element of American ska that was reflected in the music, an American variation of the Jamaican and UK rude boy—the spy.

In the 1980s, the Cold War was at its height. The U.S. boycott of the Olympic Games in Moscow in 1980 and the subsequent Soviet boycott of the Olympic Games in Los Angeles in 1984 symbolized the aggression between the two foes. Both countries experienced enormous increases in military spending as they aimed hundreds of nuclear missiles at each other. Because of the security risks, spies were used in abundance by both countries through their respective agencies, the CIA (U.S.) and the KGB (Soviet). It was a time of tumultuous relations between the countries, and popular culture reflected the political scene, with references to war, bombs, and destruction, especially in the heavy metal genre. In the ska genre, the best example of Cold War expression was the appearance of the spy, both in the music's lyrics and in the imagery and style. Although the rude boy character remained, it also morphed into the cool, sunglassed secret agent. The Toasters' song "Matt Davis Special Agent," released in 1987, set the tone. Their album, *Gun for Hire*, featured a spy on the front cover.

One might think that The Skatalites first brought spies into the ska mix with their version of the theme for James Bond, or Desmond Dekker with "007," and perhaps some bands looking to follow in the footsteps of their forefathers adopted the spy motif from these origins. But it is more likely that The Skatalites chose to cover the James Bond theme because of both the Jamaicans' affinity for American film and the fact that *Dr. No* was filmed in Jamaica in 1962 (using the well-connected Byron Lee & the Dragonaires as the scene's featured club band). Dekker likely used 007 in his song for the same reason—a fascination with American films. Certainly there was an attraction to anything cool and suave throughout ska's many eras, but in American ska, the spy, the secret agent, was especially stark and poignant against the backdrop of the Cold War.

THEMES AND COLLABORATIONS

The youth in America who comprised East Coast ska bands, as well as the fans who identified with the music, did not share the political and cultural struggles of their British predecessors. Nevertheless, working-class ethic and socialist politics crept into much of the East Coast ska repertoire. For The Toasters, such inclinations may have been carried over from Britain by Hingley, a British expatriate, but the themes played well with urban youth, even if they didn't fully understand the lyrics; they were too young to work or too entrenched in college life to know what blue-collar survival was all about. The Toasters' song "Social Security," however, still resonated with challenged youth. This song's lyrics told of a stoner high school dropout and warned about the inability to hold onto a job, girlfriend, or friends. "History Book" was a Howard Zinn-like look at the way that colonizers' histories are celebrated and the histories of slaves and the oppressed are forgotten. "Decision at Midnight" is a warning about making bad choices with alcohol, drugs, and crime, and "Haitian Frustration" even tackled international politics, railing against former Haitian dictator "Baby Doc," Jean-Claude Duvalier. The Toasters continued their proletarian themes in future years with "Don't Let the Bastards Grind You Down," an ode to the working class.

The threat of nuclear war was also a common topic for ska during this era, both in the United Kingdom and the United States, as it was in many musical genres. The Selecter's "Their Dream Goes On" and "Bombscare," both on the *Celebrate the Bullet* album, described the fear of war; Fishbone's "Party at Ground Zero," The English Beat's "Dream Home in NZ," The Specials' "Man at C&A," and The Toasters' "Radiation Skank," all foretold apocalypse from war if their warnings were not heeded.

Other songs of East Coast bands in the 1980s tackle racism, greed, power and powerlessness, wealth stratification, oppression, war, justice, and the typical themes of love and relationships, as well as providing a healthy helping of silliness and drunkenness. But this time the ills of society were seen through American eyes, focused on American issues. Shantytowns in Jamaican ska became the ghost towns in British ska and the "other side of town" in American ska.

Perhaps as an homage to its Jamaican roots, or perhaps merely as a stylistic flourish, a few ska bands of this era, and later bands, added a toaster to their tunes. This toast was frequently featured in the middle bridge of the song in place of the sax solo of the 2Tone era. It didn't occur throughout the entire song, as in Jamaican ska. The toast could be a thick Jamaican-patois line or two from an authentic Jamaican toaster, like Jack Ruby Jr. or Coolie Ranx, or a non-Jamaican with a fake accent jabbering a nonsensical slew of rhymes. Some chose to combine the Jamaican roots with the fun absurdity of British and American ska, with songs like Bim Skala Bim's "Jah Laundromat" and The Toasters' "Run Rudy Run."

OTHER BANDS AND OTHER LABELS

If one can claim that Moon Ska Records was in a way a collective for ska groups to reach their audience, one may also claim that it was paradoxically a business, a capitalistic endeavor to make money, although that was never its central focus. But without money coming in to fund the label, it simply could not exist. So as much as he was a musician, Hingley was also a businessman. The business worked somewhat like a cooperative, with profits for albums split down the middle: 50 percent for the artist, 50 percent for Moon after costs. "The Toasters were always one of the best-selling acts on the Moon Ska label and they generated enough money to allow the label to take risks on bands that were coming up," says Shafer (2012). The success of The Toasters, and the ingenuity and generosity of Hingley, helped launch the careers of dozens of bands on the Moon label.

Although The Toasters, led by Hingley, are credited with being the first to successfully market the ska sound through the Moon Ska label, others on the East Coast either serendipitously embraced the ska sound, or shortly after hearing it stateside began to produce it themselves. Bim Skala Bim from Boston formed in the same year as The Toasters, 1983. Like The Toasters, Bim Skala Bim established their own record label, first called Fonograff Records, then Razorbeat Records, then BIB. The label was formed to produce Bim Skala Bim's own music as well as others whom they signed, like Johnny Socko, Concussion Ensemble, and Bop (Harvey). It was yet another example of the DIY ethic that predominated in ska in general, as well as the American version. Bim Skala Bim helped to establish a Boston stronghold for ska music in America. They appeared on numerous compilations with a variety of other bands, and they also experienced a large number of lineup changes over their many years of seemingly endless touring. Perhaps most notable, however, is that the band linked directly to their Jamaican forefathers by working with saxophonist Roland Alphonso on a tune called "Groucho Go Ska," which introduced the Bim Skala Bim audiences to the Jamaican sounds of ska.

Another Boston staple, and possibly the best known ska band to come from the East Coast, the Mighty Mighty Bosstones formed in the early 1980s and recorded their first song in 1987 for the *Mash It Up* compilation produced by Bim Skala Bim's label, Razorbeat Records. Their name is an homage to their hometown, because it sounds like Boston, and is also a boast, reminiscent of the early stick-fighting days in Jamaica and afterward in the genre. Their first album was not released by Moon, which passed on the opportunity because the label did not have the money at the time due to distributor failures, and because Moon was more focused on traditional ska and post-2Tone sounds. Instead, the release came from Taang! Records, a local DIY label for punk and indie bands. The album, *Devil's Night Out*, was an immediate hit in the Boston underground, and touring helped to further the band's reach. In 1993, the Mighty Mighty Bosstones signed with Mercury Records on an album with a name that reflected their sound: *Ska-Core, the Devil, and More*. The band's blend of hardcore punk/rock and ska was popular with West Coast audiences and translated well to post-grunge crowds who craved a more aggressive edge. Other Boston ska bands in the 1980s included Mission Impossible, Shy Five, The Happy Campers, Class Action, and Plate O' Shrimp.

It is interesting to note that during the late 1970s and early 1980s, when the ska sounds from England came to New York, one artist was so influenced by the sound that her very first forays into performance were in a ska band. Madonna came to New York with her boyfriend, Stephen Bray, from their native Michigan, where they had formed a band called The Breakfast Club. Madonna Ciccone was their drummer. Dan Gilroy, his brother Eddie, and Angie Schmit rounded out the band, which toyed with ska. Madonna left to start her own band, Emmy & the Emmys, and also tried her hand at ska, this time on vocals with two songs, "Love on the Run" and "Simon Says."

Other East Coast bands during the 1980s stayed reasonably true to their 2Tone influences. Bigger Thomas of New Jersey, Public Service of Philadelphia, 6 Feet Under from Connecticut, The Now from Washington, D.C., and The Nails from New York (whose roadie was Jello Biafra of the Dead Kennedys prior to his fame) all created a port of entry for ska in the United States on the East Coast, and each adapted the ska sound to their own personal influences and tastes, such as punk and rock. New York also continued to churn out fantastic ska acts in the late 1980s, such as The Scofflaws and Skinnerbox.

MIDWEST SKA

Although New York and the East Coast had a vital ska scene in the 1980s, ska also found its way through the cornfields to the Midwest. In a city known for its blues, Chicago was also home to ska in its early years in the States. J. R. Jones wrote in the _Chicago Reader_: "Ever since southern jazz musicians began migrating to Chicago in the teens and 20s, the city has been a commercial clearinghouse for black music—not just jazz but blues, gospel, soul, and more recently the African and Caribbean styles marketed as 'world music'" (1998, chicagoreader.com/chicago/skas-lost-cause/content?oid=896881). Three bands brought ska to Midwest audiences in reggae clubs like the Wild Hare and Exodus, along with larger venues like the Aragon Ballroom and the Caberet Metro: Heavy Manners, the Uptown Rulers, and Rude Guest.

Heavy Manners, named after a Prince Far I album and a state of emergency declared in Jamaica in 1976, were perhaps the most recognized of the early ska bands in the Midwest. Formed in 1983, their lineup featured both black and white and both male and female members in an expression of racial unity and sexual equality. After visiting England and hearing ska, one member returned to Chicago to form the group. With their energetic sets, they opened for bands like The English Beat, The Clash, Third World, Jimmy Cliff, the Ramones, the Go Go's, Grace Jones, and Peter Tosh. It was their sold-out performance for headlining Peter Tosh at the Aragon Ballroom that helped to establish their lasting impact on the music. Tosh was so impressed with their set that he invited Heavy Manners to record with him in Chicago and later flew back from Jamaica to produce the record _Say It!_ and a number of other tracks, which were released in 2010. Heavy Manners had a sound similar to the 2Tone bands of Britain, especially because the band was formed as a direct result of hearing these bands. Videos depicting Heavy Manners are filled with skinny white neckties, Chicago mustaches, and tight white- and red-striped muscle shirts.

There were a few other bands in the Midwest during the 1980s, including Gangster Fun from Detroit, Skapone from Evanston/Chicago, and Erector Set from Cincinnati. But it wasn't until Chuck Wren founded his label devoted to Midwest ska, Jump Up!, that the music received the support that continues three decades later. Ska popped up in pockets all over the country. Florida had its own regional scene, led by Less Than Jake of Gainesville, formed in 1992.

Just as ska had blown its way up and down the East Coast and had made an appearance or two in the Midwest, it was making waves on the West Coast. Also seized by the 2Tone craze in the United Kingdom, bands in the Los Angeles area formed after their introduction to the Brits on tour. A handful of bands kicked off their own version of ska, completely different from the New York and Midwest sound.

SOUTHERN SKA

In the 1980s, a band called The Pressure Boys formed after friends at Chapel Hill High School in North Carolina were influenced by the 2Tone sound, although their songs reflected other sounds of the day, like new wave, pop, and a healthy dose of silliness. They toured the southern clubs with wild abandon and performed for college kids who craved a good time. They had success in the mid-1980s, scoring a spot on MTV for one of their videos, "Around the World," on *120 Minutes* in 1986, and opening for such bands as Duran Duran, Missing Persons, Billy Idol, REM, Bow Wow Wow, and Fishbone. They never signed to a major label although in the DIY tradition of ska, they released two EPs and an LP on their own label. In 1989, the band decided to go their own ways with members becoming a part of The Squirrel Nut Zippers, becoming music producers and label owners, becoming tour musicians for other artists, and even becoming a lawyer. They have been called the American version of Madness because of their goofy take on ska.

AMERICAN HIP-HOP ORIGINS IN JAMAICAN MUSIC

It is worth exploring the influence that Jamaican music has had on the origins of hip-hop music in the United States. Jeff Chang, in *Can't Stop Won't Stop: A History of the Hip-Hop Generation* (2005), correctly positions hip-hop's origins in Jamaica, but misses the birth. He notes that there was a black diaspora that led to the social conditions for such a creation, and he notes Edward Seaga's song contest in the 1960s, but he misses the fact that song and entertainment competitions had existed in Kingston for decades earlier with Vere Johns, and more important, he misses the act of toasting.

Toasting is the grandfather of hip-hop. It is evident that those who either participated in or witnessed the activity of toasting in the 1950s and 1960s in Kingston at the sound system dances brought this cultural phenomenon to the shores of the United States, where it then evolved into hip-hop traditions. In the 1970s, hip-hop began when a disc jockey by the stage name DJ Kool Herc began hosting block parties in the South Bronx. He, like his Jamaican predecessors, toasted over the music to encourage the attention of the participants. Hip-hop toasting then evolved into adding musical flourishes to the music, utilizing two turntables to create percussive effects like scratching and looping, and further evolved into rapping completely as a vocal, rather than a few words over the existing sound track, and vocal percussive effects, beatboxing. Hip-hop culture spread to communities throughout New York and then the world in the 1980s.

Joseph Heathcott notes the origins of hip-hop culture in Jamaica:

> Taking shape on the playgrounds and street corners of the South Bronx, hip-hop was from the first moment a popular cultural practice that stretched across borderlands, linking the local to the transnational. Not coincidentally, hop-hop erupted in the one American urban neighborhood with the highest concentration of Jamaican labor migrant families: the South Bronx. . . . Islanders imported with them to the South Bronx highly developed musical and electric performance cultures centered around the mobile sound system. If ska had filed to gain a purchase on the American music scene, and if reggae was only beginning to establish its credentials, it was the sound system and dance hall culture that ultimately made sense on transplanted soil. Where Jamaican genres of music only penetrated American markets obliquely, Jamaican performance practices provide enteral to the creation of hip-hop. (2003, p. 199)

Is it possible that DJ Kool Herc knew about these Jamaican toasting methods? Most definitely. DJ Kool Herc, whose real name is Clive Campbell, was born in 1955 in Kingston, Jamaica, where he lived until he was twelve years old, during the heyday of the sound system. He moved to the Bronx in 1967. His first gig was deejaying his sister's birthday party, and he did as he had learned, filling the break sections of the song with toasting to keep the audience going. This is not to say that DJ Kool Herc was merely imitating the originals, and indeed he was innovative, incorporating the turntables themselves in future gigs to create additional techniques that became separate from the ska genre and a part of the hip-hop genre. However, credit is due the first toasters: Count Machuki, King Stitt, and Sir Lord Comic.

EIGHT

Ska in the Key of Sunshine

The 2Tone movement in the United States had slowly simmered on the East Coast and produced a fruitful scene of its own throughout the 1980s. On the West Coast, where 2Tone bands had toured in Los Angeles, the ska sounds and style had also made an impression on youth and underground music. Fueled by the music of the United Kingdom, by soul, R& B, and the funk of Motown and Stax, along with mod and punk and heavy metal as well as the aesthetic of the cinema (in true California fashion), the West Coast blend of ska had a sound and a scene all its own. Like East Coast ska, West Coast ska could be whimsical and raucous, but it also dealt with crucial themes of racism and poverty that were uniquely Californian.

SETTING THE STAGE FOR SKA

After World War II, Los Angeles, like many other areas of the country, had racially segregated housing. Blacks and Asians suffered from racist covenants that prevented them from living in sectors of the city and the suburbs. As a result, blacks and Asians lived in the only neighborhoods that would accept them, Compton, Watts, and South and East Los Angeles. Some 95 percent of the city's housing was restricted from blacks and Asians. This pervasive racism formed the backdrop for violence two decades later. In the Watts riots in 1965, blacks fought against blatant persecution and discrimination by the LA Police Department. Years of racial injustice, beatings, criminalization, and abuse at the hands of the LAPD under police chief William Parker finally came to a head. Sparked by an incident on August 11, 1965, when a young black man was pulled over by a white California Highway Patrol motorcycle officer, the situation escalated, involving nearby witnesses. Crowds assembled, and even after the young man was arrested, along with family members who had gathered, the crowds continued to express their anger, throwing objects at the police. Crowds grew into mobs. In the ensuing days the people burned down some 1,000 buildings, assaulted police and white motorists, and expressed decades of pent-up rage over being subjugated and ostracized. More than 30,000 people took part in the riots, at the same time that the nation was experiencing the developing civil rights movement.

Even after the smoke had cleared in the years after the riots, like the low-hanging smog that plagued the city of Los Angeles, racism hung and simmered over the people, polluting society with prominently stratified distribution of wealth, sharply segregated neighborhoods, and opportunities that were available only to some, not all. Poverty increased dramatically in the 1970s and was concentrated in racial and ethnic neighborhoods. Low levels of education were endemic in these areas. To address the issues of segregation and educational deficiencies, Los Angeles, like many other large cities nationwide, adopted in 1978 a drastic desegregation plan, busing African American students to schools that were historically white. However, because neighborhoods, and thus schools, were so racially segregated, busing students to schools in the name of desegregation meant that many students had to be transported miles away from their homes, across district lines, riding on the bus for hours a day. Busing brought together the races, but created another generation of angst.

Thus, the scene was set for the political and cultural aspects of ska, which had sought to unite black and white in England. But the music that preceded ska on the West Coast gave it a different interpretation, both in its content as well as in its sound. Like British ska, West Coast ska had also evolved through punk music. The Ramones had toured Los Angeles in 1976, and The Damned came through in 1977, sparking interest in punk. Some early Los Angeles punk bands, like X, the Angry Samoans, the Germs, the Zeros, and the Avengers, were hugely influenced by the Ramones and rockabilly. Some had a novelty aspect, like The Dickies, perhaps best known for their "Banana Splits" and "Killer Klowns from Outer Space" theme songs. But the fun-loving harmonies and three-chord guitar riffs evolved in the early 1980s into a more aggressive sound as hardcore punk dominated the punk movement. Bands like the Circle Jerks and Black Flag in Los Angeles, and the Dead Kennedys and D.R.I. in San Francisco, utilized faster rhythms and heavy guitar that developed into thrash and angry lyrics. Punk gangs sprang up, especially in the Los Angeles area, and violent clashes occurred between groups such as the L.A.D.S. (LA Death Squad), L.O.D. (Lords of Destruction), and ESPs (East Side Punx). Punks also frequently clashed with police, and they had mutual hatred for each another. A police presence at shows incited further violence.

The content of punk songs was an anthem against such abuse of authority, for example in Black Flag's classic "Rise Above" and "Police

Story," as well as "Police Truck" by the Dead Kennedys and "Red Tape" by the Circle Jerks. Many punk songs were satirical in nature to prove a point, like "White Minority" by Black Flag and "Kill the Poor" by the Dead Kennedys. International topics were also fair game. Jello Biafra of the Dead Kennedys nicknamed himself as a silly matchup between something innocuous, Jell-O, and the failed secession of the state of Biafra from Nigeria in the late 1960s, which led to oppression, starvation, and death. His band sang of the naiveté, complacency, and wealth of American youth who pretended to understand revolutions in other countries, yet had not seen the real world. Others sang about forced labor and coups d'état, communism, capitalism, Reaganomics, and working all day in a cubicle.

When punk became too much, and when the violence made concerts too threatening for a segment of fans, they started to turn away from punk to music that was more convivial, but with the same vigor. They felt ostracized by punk's brutality and heavy message, delivered with fists and shouts. African Americans felt especially left out of punk's heritage because the fans and bands were almost entirely white.

MOD REVIVAL

It is not surprising that in a city of cinema, music was influenced not just by the forms that came before it or were introduced into it, but also by film. In 1979, the movie *Quadrophenia*, a British import about mod life, was billed as "a major musical statement about an angry generation is now a major motion picture for every generation," and a "triumphant answer to indifference," as the film's trailer touted. *Quadrophenia* was a film adaptation of The Who's rock opera of the same name; it featured a sound track by The Who and was produced by The Who Films. The Who had inspired the mod subculture in Britain, and *Quadrophenia* was essentially a love letter to the mods. The film featured plenty of scooters, parkas, and a glimpse of gang life, which was idealized by young Californians who enjoyed the same music and style. It even featured Sting as the main mod, Ace Face, who dances expressionless and cool in his sharkskin suit. *Quadrophenia*, at this point in California's angry punk music culture, was a respite for youths looking for another way to express their musical interests and to bond with like-minded individuals. It was a chance, not to throw fists, but to dress sharp.

Enter The Untouchables. Formed in 1981, this group with seven original members played a blend of 1960s American soul, 2Tone ska, and even a little punk, that transcended color lines and appealed to those contemptuous of mainstream rock 'n' roll, the popular power anthem arena rock of the day. Dressed in the used clothes, crombies, and pork pie hats that were fashionable with the mod set, The Untouchables got their first gig at a club of which they, and all Los Angeles mods, were patrons—the ON Klub, a venue located in Silver Lake, California, just east of Hollywood. Scooters, popular with the mod crowds, could be seen on any given night lined up outside the ON Klub, which was owned by British ex-pat Howard Paar. Paar, like Bucket of The Toasters, had a love for 2Tone ska and reggae. He regularly booked the Boxboys, an all-white ska band fronted by a female singer, Betsy Weiss, who had a big impact on The Untouchables. The Boxboys first played punk and new wave, as there was little ska in California in the late 1970s. They performed with the band Berlin, as they had the same management. They admitted that for them, ska was a rhythm they used to build their music on, and they decided to perform the sound after coming to it through reggae.

Members of The Untouchables were drawn to the Boxboys' energetic sound, upbeat tempo, and cool style. Paar gave The Untouchables a chance when they guaranteed him that they would sell out the venue, which they did. The Untouchables, akin to the punk ethic and in true American form, were independent individuals. They were similar in sound to mod bands and 2Tone bands, yet they were unlike anything else. They set the tone for being one's own, for taking a little of this and that and putting it together, like a melting pot. Drawing from their love for Motown and American R&B and British rock and soul and Jamaican ska and even psychedelic rock and pop music, The Untouchables' special blend bridged the musical divide. But they also did something even more important during this era of political and racial dissension and separation: they bridged a cultural and ethnic divide.

The Untouchables, like most of the 2Tone bands, comprised both black and white members. This was not done by design, but was organic. They all were friends. Some of the band members were neighbors in the Crenshaw neighborhood of LA. Others were friends who hung out at the same mod clubs, listened to the same mod music, wore the same military parkas, and drove the same mod Vespas. Even though some of the members couldn't even play an instrument, in their eyes they were bigger than music—they were a scene. They were mods who played ska music, and unlike the punk movement that sought to tear things down, The Untouchables and early West Coast ska preferred to build things up. They played the music of Motown, a traditionally black music, with the music of Brixton, a traditionally white music. The Untouchables didn't look like other U.S. bands of the day. They established a model—that black and white can play side by side for a crowd of blacks and whites who can dance side by side, share a drink and camaraderie side by side, and live together side by side. This was brotherhood.

PARTY AT GROUND ZERO

Influenced by similar genres, California punk and 2Tone, another band of brothers and friends came together in 1979 with a very different sound than the mod-infused ska of The Untouchables. Fishbone formed when a group of junior high school students became friends in South Central Los Angeles after they were bused to the same school through desegregation efforts in the 1970s. Brothers John Norwood Fisher and Phillip "Fish" Fisher were the nucleus of the band, joined by Angelo Moore, Kendall Jones, "Dirty" Walter A. Kibby II, and Christopher Dowd.

The band was its own blend. As music critic Stephen Thomas Erlewine put it, Fishbone were "equal parts of deep funk, high-energy punk, and frantic ska," but they also threw in a healthy helping of hard rock and metal at times, giving some songs a decidedly darker sound in later years. Fishbone were definitely a live band. Lead vocalist and saxophonist Angelo Moore, who went by the nickname Dr. Madd Vibe, stirred up the band's special concoction and the audience's reaction with his hyperactive acrobatics on stage and into the audience, wearing no shirt and with baggy trousers held up only by thin suspenders. Norwood's single giant dreadlock at the front of his head propelled the mythical image of this "all-black odd ball crew," as they were called by Nathan Brackett of *Rolling Stone*. Their frenzied performances were matched only by their eclectic sound, which appealed to both black and white audiences. As a result, like East Coast ska, marketers weren't sure where to put Fishbone, so they lumped them in with "alternative" rock. This, however, was not a bad move for Fishbone.

Fishbone could play in Peoria, as the saying goes, because they had crossover appeal. They could be funk, they could be rock, they could be ska, and in fact they were all of these things, so they appeared on concert bills with a variety of acts and were thus introduced to a wide audience. They performed with such bands as Run D.M.C., the Red Hot Chili Peppers, the Dead Kennedys, Bad Manners, Jane's Addiction, the Beastie Boys (on their License to Ill tour), Living Colour, Public Enemy, Thelonius Monster, REM, Elvis Costello, Primus, X, and Rollins Band. Their musical diversity, musical eccentricities, could be too much to get a firm grip on at times. Not being able to fit neatly into a category also meant not being able to find a niche, so Fishbone suffered for their broad strokes of sound. They were never able to fully capture the success of their talent.

The topics of their songs were almost as eclectic as their music. Like many ska bands before them, they sang about ska itself, the lack of radio play for ska, and the power of ska to elevate one's mood. Lyrics made reference to rude boys and rude girls and skanking. There was also a lot of sex and whores and blatant references to genitalia as well as the innuendo found in calypso, and plenty of boasting, too. But Fishbone also sang of dark social ills. They sang of crack addiction that spread across class and neighborhood lines; poverty in the inner city; winos and the mentally ill; divorce and its impact on children; questioning authority and bureaucracy and the frivolity of society; racism, alcoholism, war, religion, and depression. There were biblical references. They sang with sarcasm, with irony. Songs like "It's a Wonderful Life (Gonna Have a Good Time)" were about poverty and death. "Party at Ground Zero" tells of war that destroys the entire planet. "Freddie's Dead," the classic Curtis Mayfield song, is about a man with no options in life, abused by life—that's it, no happy ending. With such upbeat tempos, fast rhythms, layered sounds, and rapid lyrics, it was sometimes easy to miss what the songs were saying. The words were very dark, and the commentary was very sharp. This was the same message delivered by hardcore punk, but without the constant screaming. It was angry without the destruction, and it offered listeners a chance to think about the issues more critically, calling the problems into question for themselves, deconstructing events and history in a way that laid the subject bare.

Fishbone, as much as they had crossover appeal for white audiences, were every bit a black band. Their racial makeup, their content, celebrated the African American artist. Scholar Trey Ellis comments:

> I now know that I am not the only black person who sees the black aesthetic as much more than just Africa and jazz. Finally finding a large body of like-minded armors me with the nearly undampenable enthusiasm of the born again. And my friends and I—a minority's minority mushrooming with the current black bourgeoisie boom—I have inherited an open-ended New Black Aesthetic from a few Seventies pioneers that shamelessly borrows and reassembles across both race and class lines. . . . Brought together by court-ordered busing out to a mostly white San Fernando Valley junior high school, the six members are the New Black Aesthetic personified. They are a mongrel mix of classes and types, and their political music sounds out this hybrid. (1989, p. 234)

OTHER BANDS

The Untouchables broke up in 1984 after the members of the original lineup each went a different direction musically. Fishbone still perform despite self-destructing when Kendall Jones had a nervous breakdown and fled for his father's religious cult, causing Norwood and others to stage an intervention, which landed them in court on kidnapping charges. Still, these two bands were essential not only in bringing ska to the West Coast and raising awareness of critical issues, especially racism, but also for their influence on countless others. The liner notes for The Untouchables' album *Cool Beginnings*, a collection of their early work, sum up their influence: "Color barriers were smashed as black and white youths came from neighboring cities and counties to join the mod revival in unity, harmony and ska. 1983 was a very good year for ska mods in Hollywood." Other bands followed suit, bringing together large audiences no matter what their color or background.

One of those bands, No Doubt, took ska in the direction of pop music to appeal to more mainstream audiences, with their wallet chains and skater looks. As a result, they had huge commercial appeal, and their music strayed from their ska roots into big energy arena pop. Influenced by Madness, No Doubt formed in Anaheim in 1987. They first performed on a bill with fourteen other bands, opening for The Untouchables in Long Beach, California. After lead singer John Spence committed suicide, backup singer Gwen Stefani stepped up to fill the position as lead vocalist and head glamour puss. Eric Stefani, Gwen's older brother and the band's founder and songwriter, also left the band to pursue a career as an animator. Their song "Everything's Wrong" appeared on the Moon Ska Records compilation *Ska Face* in 1988, a compilation that debuted many national acts, not just East Coast bands. They were firmly planted in the ska scene and opened for the popular West Coast bands of the day, like the Red Hot Chili Peppers and Ziggy Marley and the Melody Makers. Despite the appeal of grunge during the early 1990s and not receiving any radio play, No Doubt continued to gain in popularity by playing live shows. Although many of their songs have no ska sound at all, many still employ the ska beat, such as the popular "Just a Girl" and the funkier, brassier "Spiderwebs." The band's image utilizes their 2Tone influences, with black and white checked garb and suspenders. They covered ska tunes from their favorite 2Tone bands, and even The Skatalites, during their live sets.

Although many ska traditionalists verbally flogged No Doubt over the years for their appeal to the mainstream, without No Doubt, other bands and other fans would never have been drawn to ska's roots. They opened up a new audience of young minds to the rhythms and styles of ska and went on to bigger success in the 1990s, taking ska along with them for the ride. Their lyrics tended to stick to the topics of love and love lost and love shunned, and only "once in a while" would they "sit back and think about the planet," as Stefani sang. They weren't singing about the Cold War or racism or unemployment as others had; instead, they appealed to those looking for the good time ska and pop that made people dance and party. Stefani once said that their songs were about having fun and not getting too deep.

Operation Ivy's story is briefly chronicled in the song "Journey to the End of East Bay," by Rancid, the band that formed with members Tim Armstrong and Matt Freeman after Operation Ivy's breakup. Operation Ivy formed at Berkeley in 1987 and began performing at 924 Gilman Street, a club that helped give them their start, along with other well-known groups like Green Day. Membership was a collective effort in the not-for-profit club, so decisions were made by the whole. The club also endorsed straightedge philosophy—no drugs, no alcohol, no racism, no violence—and was considered sacred ground. Straightedge was a subculture of hardcore punk with teetotaling values that originated in the early 1980s with Minor Threat on the East Coast and quickly spread.

Named after American nuclear tests in the weapons race with the Soviet Union, Operation Ivy, though not exactly a straightedge band, did sing about the culture shared by this music, such as unity, peace, equality, teenage angst, and existential angst. They may have been sharing topics with some bands on the West Coast who dared to delve into the deeper issues, but they only hit the surface with broad strokes of statements, instead of gritty firsthand experience. But the message was heard by their audience of devotees and their sound, which was a sparse blend of pop punk and ska, featured the rhythmic strums of ska guitar and the convivial energy that had always been a part of ska music. Their logo had a ska look, a black and white guy with a pork pie hat, which was designed by singer Jesse Michael. A number of their songs reflected ska themes, like "Sound System" and "Unity." They brought ska to white college students in a way that communicated to them—through punk.

In 1985, Donkey Show began playing their brand of ska in San Diego. Founded by legendary saxophonist Dave Hillyard, who went on to play with bands such as Hepcat, The Slackers, and his own collectives, Donkey Show featured both female and male vocalists. They performed on the West Coast with Fishbone and others and then in the late 1980s they toured the East Coast, performing with The Toasters. They spread the ska sound throughout the country with stops in places like Omaha, Youngstown, St. Louis, and Houston. They split in 1990 when Hillyard went to play with Hepcat.

After seeing The English Beat perform in San Francisco in 1981, The Uptones were formed by three high school friends from Berkeley. They went by two different names at first—Hobo, then Stiff Richards. Their sound was strictly 2Tone, although they added in a little mod and punk at times. Their sets were energetic, and because the members of the band were only in their mid-teens when they started, the audiences were young as well, mostly high school students who stage dived and moshed to the tunes.

Let's Go Bowling came onto the ska scene in 1986 with an ample horn section to punctuate their traditional style. But it wasn't until 1991 that they recorded their first full-length CD, *Music to Bowl By*, which was released on Moon Ska Records. With eight original members, including a toaster, they were a large ensemble, as many ska bands were. Their sound was more akin to The Skatalites than to their West Coast contemporaries, especially the Latin-inspired tunes. Just ahead of the swing curve that would circle back around in the mid-1990s, Let's Go Bowling incorporated jazzy, big-band melodies with three-part vocal harmonies. They were nothing like the hardcore punk scene that had preceded many other ska bands in the region, instead taking their influences from the root—Jamaican jazz.

Also founded in 1986, The Skeletones from Riverside, California, featured a lineup of both black and white members. Their repertoire included jazz, soul, and reggae as well as their main sound, ska, and they performed with such bands as the Red Hot Chili Peppers, Fishbone, Echo and the Bunnymen, and Bad Religion. They appeared on numerous compilations while also releasing a small number of albums of their own. In true ska style, they started their own label to release their material, MJC. Their songs "Nutty Day" and "The Telephone" were true to their British ska influence.

In 1991, nearly a decade after ska arrived on the West Coast, Easy Big Fella began performing ska in Seattle, right around the same time that grunge made a big splash. They opened for bands like The Skatalites, The Specials, Desmond Dekker, and The Toasters, but didn't produce their first album, *Easy Listening*, until 1994. They became part of a movement, and of course a compilation, known as Big Foot Ska—ska from Bigfoot country, Oregon, Washington, and British Columbia. Other bands from this region included Cherry Poppin' Daddies, Franceska, The Readymen, Engine 54, and The Investigators, as every nook and cranny of the country developed its own scene.

Like Los Angeles, San Jose was also a center of ska in the late 1980s. Skankin' Pickle performed regularly at clubs around the city and the region. Formed in 1988 by schoolmates from Westmont High School and Los Gatos High School, the group began as a five-piece band and added a sixth member in 1990. A year later, in true DIY style, they formed their own record label, Dill Records, to release their own material. Their first album comprised both live tracks and studio recording and was aptly titled *Skafunkrastapunk*, a title indicative of ska music in America during this era. It was a blend of styles, of influences. The band stuck to their independent values and would only perform at all-ages shows with low cover charges, and they only sold their CDs for half of what CDs cost in chain stores.

Perhaps the most notable of Skankin' Pickle's influences on the ska industry was vocalist and saxophonist Mike Park. Park began distributing records in 1991 while a member of Skankin' Pickle, but in 1996 he went on to begin his own label, Asian Man Records, which he still runs from his garage. The label supports ska and punk bands that are not racist, sexist, or prejudiced. A number of bands have found success through Park's label, including Lawrence Arms, Less Than Jake, MU330, and Alkaline Trio. Park became involved in political causes through his label. In 1999, he formed a group called Plea for Peace Foundation to promote peace through music.

But most recognizable is Park's creation of the Ska Against Racism tour, which he started in the spring of 1998 as a way to raise awareness of racism and raise funds for antiracist causes and groups. Park, a Korean American, felt the effects of racism when four Nazis attended one of his Skankin' Pickle concerts in 1991 and began sieg heiling. The first lineup at the Ska Against Racism tour was Less Than Jake, MU330, The Toasters, Five Iron Frenzy, Blue Meanies, and Mustard Plug. Unfortunately, after a few years the tour had raised very little money for organizations, just over $20,000, and the crowds were not receptive to the message. In fact, most bands did little to discuss racism on stage, and if they did, the crowds, largely white, hostilely booed or cursed them. After the invasion of Iraq, the tour merged with Plea for Peace, which became a music tour of its own.

THEMES

As noted previously, Fishbone's music was heavy with social themes like race, poverty, and authority, but a number of West Coast bands also tapped into these topics. The Untouchables' "The General" referenced the military machine that was prevalent during the 1980s and mocked its power. Their song "Lebanon" also discussed the stupidity of war and a soldier who has been deployed there with no knowledge of the purpose of the mission. In the song, the soldier kills a man he doesn't know and realizes that this is wrong; he is afraid he too will die. "Mandingo" was a fictional rudeboy character The Untouchables created for their song of the same name, which told the story with a spaghetti Western flavor. "Government Don't Need Nobody" was about a power structure that doesn't think with the heart and instead is fueled by money.

The spy references and images used in East Coast ska also appeared on the West Coast, likely influenced by the same rude boy meets Cold War mix. The Untouchables' 1988 album *Agent Double O Soul* and their now-classic song "I Spy (for the FBI)," and Let's Go Bowling's "Spy Market" are a few examples. Operation Ivy's ska man logo has a spy feel to it. There were also plenty of references to the original rude boys of Jamaica and the stylized version in England. The cover of The Untouchables' *Wild Child* album features a rude boy, lead vocalist Tony Rugolo himself, in a pork pie hat and darkers.

On the West Coast, probably because of the large Latino population, Latin themes and sounds began to pop up in ska music. The Cuban connection in Jamaica had done it one generation earlier with "Latin Goes Ska" and plenty of Mongo Santamaria tunes, and in Los Angeles the influence of Mexican immigrants on the music was the same. The Voodoo Glow Skulls, who didn't actually come onto the West Coast scene until 1988, were originally a hardcore group. Three Riverside brothers, Frank, Jorge, and Eddie Casillas, founded the group with a friend before adding a horn section to the mix a few years later. Their first album, *Who Is, This Is?*, featured plenty of one- and two-minute-long, rapid-fire songs, blending punk with ska, as well as a song sung entirely in Spanish. Their second album, *Firme*, featured releases both entirely in English and entirely in Spanish. They continued to release both English and Spanish songs in a style whose name they coined in the title of one of their later albums, *California Street Music*. Other bands on the West Coast in the early 1990s combined ska and Latin sounds as well, like Los Hooligans, Orixa, Slow Gherkin, and Yeska.

THE HOLLYWOOD CONNECTION

West Coast ska bands also found a calling that could only be realized in the land of Tinseltown—cinema. For the first time, ska bands began to appear in movies as well as on their sound tracks. The Untouchables have a cameo scene in *Repo Man*, the 1984 cult classic directed by Alex Cox, in which they appear as a scooter gang. They were a bit typecast, perhaps, and they didn't have a musical number, but this wasn't their only appearance on celluloid. They also were featured as a club band in 1987's *No Man's Land*, they performed their song "The General" for the 1984 comedy *Party Animal*, and they appeared as themselves in the movie *Surf II*, spoofing the Annette Funicello and Frankie Avalon beach party movies. This spoof was taken a step further by Fishbone, who performed a silly rendition of "Jamaica Ska" (the tune Byron Lee & the Dragonaires brought to the 1964 World's Fair) with Annette and Frankie in the 1987 sequel *Back to the Beach*. Fishbone also had tunes on a number of movie sound tracks, including *Say Anything, I'm Gonna Git You Sucka, Tapeheads*, and *The Mask*, to name a few. They also had cameos in the Eurythmics video for "Would I Lie to You." Their music has been played everywhere from Disney movies to the Playboy mansion. Of course Gwen Stefani of No Doubt has risen to celebrity status, with cameos in Martin Scorsese's *The Aviator*, playing Jean Harlow, and in *Zoolander*, along with creating her own fashion lines and fragrance.

Ska bands also made plenty of appearances on national television shows. In 1991, Fishbone appeared on *Saturday Night Live* and gave energetic performances of their songs "Sunless Saturday" and "Everyday Sunshine." They also performed on *Soul Train, Late Night with Conan O'Brien*, and the *Late Late Show with Craig Kilborn*. No Doubt has performed on *Saturday Night Live* three times, as well as on the *Ellen DeGeneres Show, American Idol, Dawson's Creek, The Tonight Show with Jay Leno, MADtv*, the *MTV Video Music Awards*, and *MTV TRL*. The Mighty Mighty Bosstones have performed on the *Late Late Show with Craig Kilborn, Late Show with David Letterman, Jimmy Kimmel Live*, and even *Beavis and Butthead* and other MTV shows like *120 Minutes* and *Reverb*. Their song "The

Impression That I Get" was featured in the Activision game *Band Hero*, as were No Doubt's "Don't Speak" and "Just a Girl."

Why is this fusion between ska and Hollywood important? First, it was natural for music and movies to mix because of the nature of the industry. Popular music makes its way onto sound tracks as a way to appeal to the emotions and interests of the viewer. Associating movies with their sound tracks is a powerful link, as any fan of John Hughes's many music-laden films will agree. But there was also the need for ska bands on the West Coast to extend their reach, and therefore their worth. Reaching bigger audiences through an entirely separate medium was an important factor in the bands' survival and commercial success. It also lent legitimacy to the genre as a whole, demonstrating that movie producers and the advertising industry saw the value of the music. It wasn't just an underground sound or a passing fad, but something more, something stronger, something that had the potential to make it big.

Whether blended with punk, mod, funk, rock, or pop, or just returning to its roots, West Coast ska had a common experimental and independent spirit. Ska bands on the West Coast, East Coast, and throughout the country that formed and performed in the 1980s and were able to last were at the forefront of the mid-1990s ska boom in the United States. This version of the music featured even more interpretations and reinterpretations of not only ska and punk, but virtually every other musical genre. If only ska bands could find a medium of communication beyond the stage.

MTV AND THE POWER OF MUSIC VIDEO

MTV first came to television on August 1, 1981, bringing a whole new dimension to music—the visual. During the British era of ska, MTV was still in its infancy, and as such tended to ignore the genre in favor of what was already popular in the United States throughout the 1980s, music from the likes of Madonna, Flock of Seagulls, A-Ha, Duran Duran, Dire Straits, Michael Jackson, and Tina Turner. "In the early days of MTV, music videos became a vehicle to revive veteran rock stars like Rod Stewart and promote hot, new acts like The Stray Cats" ("MTV Changed the Music Industry" 1998).

But bands like Madness, The Specials, and The English Beat also made music videos, because promo videos aired on BBC. And these videos aired on MTV, albeit not in the normal rotation and not until years later, on shows late at night that contained either music from England or alternative music, like *120 Minutes*. Dave Wakeling remembers filming two videos for one song because the video for British audiences was deemed too risqué for American viewers, dealing with a gender-bending theme, although a sexist image of a writhing blonde beauty on a bed was perfectly acceptable. He says that music video producers also made sure to give him eye drops to make his blue eyes even bluer, because it was not their music that would sell to U.S. markets, but their sex appeal.

After MTV took over American pop culture in the 1980s, exposure of one's music video in the 1990s was almost essential for survival. Producing a high-quality film, which is in essence what a music video was, and having the clout and commercial appeal to secure a slot in rotation on MTV was a formula for success. Because producing a video of this nature required considerable cash, and obtaining the slot to air the video was next to impossible without capital backing from a large label, most ska bands in the 1990s either did not produce music videos at all, or if they did, those videos never saw the light of day. There were a few exceptions, like some put out by The Toasters, Mighty Mighty Bosstones, No Doubt, and a handful of others, which were rarely seen. The ska videos that aired on MTV appeared during a show called *Buzz Bin*, which was dedicated to up-and-coming artists, even though many of the bands had been around a decade or more at that point; they were new or promising bands in the eyes of the viewing public and the industry/MTV. These were bands that were "buzzworthy." The impact that music video had on ska was to give a few bands the attention they strove for and others craved. The lack of attention from the music video industry revealed that American ska music was still considered an underground genre. But ska had always been a DIY genre, and with or without the support of corporate cable television, ska would find success of its own.

NINE

Ska Boom and Ska Bust

Ska music reached its cultural height in Jamaica and England as a result of oppressive conditions. It offered an exultant escape. Its next period of growth was no different. An economic recession plagued the United States after the largest stock market crash in history occurred on Black Monday in October 1987, when the Dow lost $500 million in value. *Time* magazine proclaimed on its cover, "After a wild week on Wall Street the world is different" (Nov. 2, 1987). World markets plummeted in response, and although the cause was debated by economists, the effects felt by the world were the same: uncertainty reigned in the markets.

Then at the end of 1990, in what would become the First Gulf War, U.S. troops entered Kuwait in an attempt to remove Iraqi forces from the oil-rich land they had invaded. In February 1991, the United States, along with coalition forces, began a series of air attacks against Iraq. It was another uncertain time, as the world watched America's involvement in the Middle East and wondered if this was the beginning of the end. When over a half million U.S. troops left Kuwait for home in March 1991, after driving out Iraqi forces, the Iraqi military set fire to the oil fields of Kuwait, scorching the earth for eleven months at a cost of $1.5 billion to Kuwait in lost oil and releasing an unquantifiable amount of pollution into the ozone layer, causing permanent damage. The world would once again never be the same.

Young Americans felt disenfranchised by the imperialistic direction of the country and their own lack of opportunity. Generation X, as they were labeled, became apathetic about their prospects in life. Whereas ska music had a small underground following who were not specifically expressing the larger social malaise, the new genre of grunge did speak to these cultural forces directly and in turn helped ska to live on and even thrive.

GRUNGE

The minor chords, the scuzzy guitar, the screaming voice wailing long, drawn-out notes portending agony and dirt. Greasy locks flailing around seas of plaid shirts tied around ripped jeans. Too apathetic to tie the unlaced Docs slipped on for a night of drinking cheap beer. This was grunge. Was there anything else in the early 1990s? Seattle was the town that everybody loved, and the music was full of rot. Generation X flocked to the sound, angry at corporate culture and the military machine that the country had become, unconcerned about their future, and snidely irritated at pop culture. Bands such as Nirvana, Soundgarden, Pearl Jam, Smashing Pumpkins, Alice in Chains, Stone Temple Pilots, and Mudhoney attracted antiestablishment, defiant, DIY teenagers, the same philosophies that permeated the punk and mod movements. But grunge, unlike punk and mod, never attracted the same crowd as ska, even though they were all lumped into the same category of "alternative" by the music industry. And musically, grunge was the antithesis of ska, in tone, tempo, and energy. So how then did grunge contribute to ska's prospering in the years that followed the grunge bubble?

The feel of grunge was heavy, both aesthetically and spiritually. Its mood permeated many other genres, featuring bloated, brusque vocals and distorted and thick guitars. It simply became too much. It was too weighty, too depressing, and too dark. MTV was showing images of child abuse and children bullying each other to the point of violence, and grunge's lyrics of homelessness, mental illness, blood, excrement, sweat, death, suffering, and molestation were too troubling to most viewers. Grunge couldn't last for long, and in its most intense form it didn't. Even those who once loved the genre had to get away, for fear of otherwise crawling into a hole and dying.

As grunge music began to wane, especially after the death of Nirvana's Kurt Cobain, who had become its idol-turned-martyr, the void that was left beckoned for something brighter. Ska had solid followings on the East and West Coasts, in the Midwest, and in regional pockets of the United States, and when grunge's candle burnt out, the opportunity for ska to finally go mainstream emerged.

SKA BOOM

Many of the ska bands that came through the door left open by grunge vacating the industry were its opposite: saccharinely sweet, poppy, silly, and catchy pop acts. But others were continuing the music they had been playing all along during the 1980s, and they finally got a larger following. Larger labels started to sign ska bands during the mid-1990s, radio began to play songs by ska bands, MTV finally aired ska videos in the normal rotation and during shows like *120 Minutes,* and businesses started to see that there was an opportunity for marketing their goods to the youths who frequented ska concerts.

"Five years ago, ska concerts in Manhattan were strictly underground events, where green-haired punks, skinheads and stylish ska fans known as rude boys danced to the holy triumvirate of New York ska bands: the Toasters, the Scofflaws and the N.Y. Citizens," wrote *New York Times* journalist Neil Strauss in 1997. "Now there are concerts every weekend at downtown clubs like Wetlands, New Music Cafe, the Cooler and Coney Island High, and the audience is a broad, multi-racial mix, where hippies meet skinheads and college jocks dance with rude boys" (p. 137). Tony Kanal, bassist for one of the most successful bands to come out of the ska industry, No Doubt, also noticed the change in audience, which helped propel his band to stardom. Rock critic Greg Kot wrote of Kanal: "Ten years ago he was playing it for a few hundred people in Los Angeles clubs. Two weeks ago his band's ska-tinged pop brought a crowd of more than 20,000 fans mostly screaming teens and adolescents, to the World Music Theatre." Kanal commented, "Alternative-rock kids are buying this music now, not just the rude boys and rude girls who used to show up at shows riding their Vespas. Five years ago we made a record and nobody outside our scene noticed because it came out when grunge was taking off with Nirvana, Pearl Jam. But the musical climate has changed, and people are looking for some happier music" (1997, Tempo, p. 1).

One of the outlets that helped ska to reach more ears, in addition to the proliferation of zines, was college radio. This was a direct link to the audience that resonated most with newly emerging ska bands. Steve Shafer (2012) of Moon Ska Records recalls, "At the time there were about 10 college radio stations that were getting our stuff sporadically. Soon, anything that came out, we sent out promo copies. Music directors, DJs, or just a kid who had a ska show or a show that played ska, got in touch with us and we sent materials. We put it in our newsletter for college radio and DJs to get in touch with us."

Northwestern University radio station WNUR-FM 89.3 debuted a one-hour weekly ska show in the early 1990s. Host Chuck Wren used this platform to launch his own ska label in 1993, Jump Up! Records, and virtually single-handedly promoted the Midwest collective of ska bands. Wren helped to promote and release work from such bands as Deal's Gone Bad, Heavy Manners, Skapone, and Green Room Rockers in addition to a number of European artists over the years. In 1990, KUCI-FM 88.9 at the University of California Irvine began its weekly *Ska Parade* show, which played music, both live and recorded, from regional acts during their infancy, such as No Doubt, Let's Go Bowling, Goldfinger, the Aquabats, and Sublime. Brothers Bradford Stein and Brett Stein, who go by the pseudonyms Tazy Phillipz and Albino Brown, respectively, were effective promoters of these bands' efforts.

Many other college radio stations had their own shows, including *Identity Skarisis"* on WKDU at Drexel University in Philadelphia and *Rude Radio* on KUOM (Radio K) at the University of Minnesota in Minneapolis, where historian and filmmaker Brad Klein brought ska to the region, along with Evan Pedersen and Courtney Klos in later years.

Television also started to include more ska music in the repertoire of music videos. Both MTV and VH1 included ska in their normal rotations, back in the days when these stations actually showed music videos. Save Ferris's cover of "Come on Eileen"; the Mighty Mighty Bosstones' "The Impression That I Get"; Reel Big Fish's "Sell Out"; The Toasters' "Two Tone Army"; Goldfinger's "Here in Your Bedroom"; No Doubt's "Just a Girl," "Spiderwebs," and "Don't Speak"; and Fishbone's "Party at Ground Zero" are a few of the ska songs that received airplay on MTV. Many bands performed live on late-night television shows like *The Arsenio Hall Show, Late Night with Conan O'Brien,* and *Late Show with David Letterman.*

Many of the bands that utilized the ska sound might not have been ska bands at all, and instead were pop bands that added a ska flourish, an occasional ska beat or a horn bridge, to a song to give it a little flavor. These bands received even bigger airplay on radio and MTV. Bands like Smashmouth, Sugar Ray, Cherry Poppin' Daddies, Squirrel Nut Zippers, and Sublime capitalized on the trend. Many bands kept one foot firmly rooted in pop or alternative music to be easily classified by the industry, which still had a hard time placing ska in a category despite its popularity.

Those who were not afraid to classify themselves as ska went on tour with like bands, performing on a bill with five or six bands a night. Shafer says this was done because of critical mass. If fans came to see one band, chances are they would hear a new band they also liked and buy their CD as a result. "You couldn't sell if you didn't tour. You could guarantee maybe selling 10,000 to 15,000 CDs if you were a good band, but if you were willing to tour, the sales were much higher. Every band we signed, we stressed they had to tour. The Toasters took them out on tour and after that they were on their own. Bands like Spring Heeled Jack, Skavoovie & the Epitones, always did better when they toured. Record stores placed enormous orders for everything in our catalogue. You could go into any record store and find our stuff. Tower Records and Coconuts would have it. It shouldn't be there and that's where it was," says Shafer (2012).

Ska bands cropped up everywhere. Any kid who was in a high school jazz band assembled a ska band with his five or ten closest friends and played faster and tighter than anything that came before them, with tempo changes, rhythm changes, and key changes. "These groups sometimes find older players from the jazz or Latin music worlds; other times they recruit young people who have just graduated from their high school jazz band" (Strauss, 1997, p. 138). They coined amusing names for their bands that utilized the word ska, such as Jimmy Skafa, Skapone, Ska Capella, The Skadfathers, The Skadolescents, The Skalapenos, Skamakaze, Issac Green and the Skalars, and Skali Baba and the Forty Ounce Horns. Others were just as clever, like the Skeletones, the Mosquitones, and the Decapitones. "The word 'ska' can be combined with almost anything," writes Strauss. "There have been Skalapalooza tours and Skampilation records; this weekend, there's a Skalloween concert in the East Village, and in December New York is to have its first Skanukkah concert" (1995, p. 139). Crowds were eclectic, as a result of the exposure in various settings with various other acts: old people, young people, skaters, hippies, punks, stoners, metalheads, nerds, skins, and the traditional ska fan decked out in garb reminiscent of the 2Tone era.

There were as many styles of ska as there were ska bands, as each group interpreted it in their own way. Subgenres of ska included skacore; Latin ska; traditional ska; ska funk; skacid, which is inspired by house music; swing ska; acoustic ska; klezmer ska; and even Christian ska, performed by The Insyderz, The O. C. Supertones, and Five Iron Frenzy. Ska blended with virtually every other genre of music and was truly an American melting pot of styles: funk, jazz, soul, rock, heavy metal, punk, pop, swing, folk, and more. It could be found alongside Oi! and punk shows and on compilations, as the music appealed to both audiences. There was even an Oi! Ska Festival in 1994. There was also theater ska from the likes of the Aquabats, who wore costumes while performing. "The band is known for their elaborate mythology. Led by MC Bat Commander, the Aquabats are superheroes on an epic quest to stop evil through the power of music. This mythology is carried over to their outrageous live performances where the band members dress as superheroes and battle super villains on stage" (BGSU Lib Guides, n.d.).

Those who were "traditionalists" and preferred their ska as true to its Jamaican roots as possible, following such bands as the Slackers, the Scofflaws, the Allstonians, Jump With Joey, The New York Ska Jazz Ensemble, Hepcat, and The Toasters, waged a phantom feud with those who savored other formations and concoctions. Hepcat, specifically, sounded more akin to the ska vocals and rocksteady of the Jamaican era. Led by two vocalists, Greg Lee and Alex Desért, Hepcat's sound was soulful and reminiscent of American R&B. Their album *Right on Time* contained songs that told a story, one after another, like a neat musical book. Their 2000 album *Push'N Shove* predated No Doubt's album of the same name by more than a decade. They felt that much of the commercialization of ska had resulted in watering down its authentic sound. "There are all these bands doing a little ska in another sound. I wondered why they just don't become a funk band if they are playing ska and fun, or why not just become a punk band if they are playing ska and punk?" questioned Lee (quoted in McLennan, 1998, p. C5). Hepcat adds calypso flourishes to their music as well, and they have worked with Jamaican greats Sly & Robbie and Buju Banton for a traditional sound.

Every metropolitan area had its own ska scene. Clubs booked multiple bands on one bill, leading to the cross-pollination of sounds. Just as fans clung to their ska styles as a badge to wear on their sleeves, they also touted their regional roots, again creating a rivalry among comrades. Even Utah had a huge ska scene, popular among Mormons for its message of love and unity, which is the subject of Brandon Smith's 2008 documentary *The Up Beat*.

The music industry saw the potential for sales, and corporations did as well. Businesses began sponsoring bands on tour. Some of the tours became like corporations themselves, like Lollapalooza, which booked many ska acts, and the Vans Warped Tour. Some of The Toasters' music was used on advertisements for Coca-Cola, AOL, and on a Nickelodeon show called *Kablaam*. At one point, The Toasters had sponsorships and partnerships from Conn-Selmer wind instruments, Ludwig drum, Jagermeister, Ska Brewing, Pick World, Ernie Ball, Greasy Groove, Reverend Guitars, and Instanbul Cymbals. These sponsorships were for the most part music related. Other bands were sponsored by shoe companies, radio stations, MTV, clothing companies, collection services, video gaming corporations, magazines, extreme sports companies, beverage companies, the auto industry, and more. With tours like the Vans Warped Tour, which booked ska bands like the Voodoo Glow Skulls, No Doubt, Sublime, Reel Big Fish, Save Ferris, the Mighty Mighty Bosstones, the Pietasters, Less Than Jake, and Hepcat, ska experienced a crossover to the skater crowd, further expanding its reach. AirWalk and Kit Kat used ska from the band Out of Order in their advertising campaigns.

"Ska is probably the biggest underground network going right now," said Fred Feldman, the general manager of Another Planet records. "Moon Records has a 15,000-name direct-marketing list, and the Toasters are selling at least 25,000 to 30,000 records now, most of it through non-traditional retail outlets. I think the bigger labels are still waiting to see what happens with this Rancid song and to see how Green Day does with the ska band it signed to its 510 label, the Dancehall Crashers. If any of it becomes huge, then you'll see a feeding frenzy" (quoted in Strauss, 1997, p. 138).

More labels, such as Heartbeat, Jump Up! Records, Beloved Entertainment, Asian Man Records, Steady Beat Recordings, Stomp Records, Hellcat, and Stubborn Records, started to devote themselves to ska bands, both new and old. Big labels took notice also, wanting to cash in on the movement. Capitol Records, Mercury Records, MCA, and Epic all began to sign ska bands. Shafer (2012) remembers when The Toasters were courted by a big label:

Around 1996, Mercury Records was sniffing around and had one of the A&R guys follow the Toasters around for a couple of months and we had meetings with the head of Mercury Records. They wanted to sign the Toasters and they kind of wanted to make the Toasters the next Bosstones in terms of attention. But one of the parts of the deal, because we didn't want to rob Moon of one of their biggest acts, was to distribute Moon's other titles. But it got weird because if we put all of the balls into their basket, they would control it all and make it or break it. So the deal fell apart. Bucket didn't want to kill the label for the Toasters' success. He said no. Bucket's motives were good and right. I completely respect his decision.

Other bands did sign with big labels and found commercial success; major magazines' headlines proclaimed that ska was the "next big thing." The Mighty Mighty Bosstones signed with Mercury Records, and soon their songs were featured in movies, such as *Clueless* with Alicia Silverstone; on television for a performance on *Sesame Street's Elmopalooza*, whose sound track garnered a Grammy Award, and on *Saturday Night Live*; in the game *Band Hero*; and on a Converse commercial. No Doubt signed with Trauma Records, a division of Interscope Records, and then after a lawsuit, signed directly with Interscope. Their songs appeared on sound tracks for movies such as *Go*, *Rugrats*, and *Zoolander*, and on television in *Dawson's Creek* and *Gossip Girl*. Their songs are also featured in the game *Band Hero*, which was the subject of a lawsuit, and singer Gwen Stefani has reached celebrity status with her clothing lines, perfume, and numerous print and broadcast commercials. They have collaborated with some of the biggest names in music, including Prince and Elvis Costello, and Jamaican artists Toots Hibbert, Sly & Robbie, Bounty Killer, Lady Saw, and Busy Signal.

No Doubt's collaborations with Jamaican artists were a nod to the roots of the ska they peppered their tunes with, and they even recorded most of their album *Rocksteady* in Jamaica, two hours north of Kingston in Port Antonio. This was not the only acknowledgment of ska's roots. Many other bands either covered Jamaican ska originals or toured or recorded with Jamaican pioneers. The Skatalites, who had performed a reunion show at the Sunsplash festival in Montego Bay in 1983, reformed in the United States in the late 1980s and started touring the States and Europe in the early 1990s. In 1993, they recorded *Skavoovie*, their first album as a reunited group. They embarked on a tour to promote the album with ska bands of all eras, including Special Beat (members of The Specials and The Beat), The Selecter, and The Toasters. The Skatalites were still touring and producing albums of new material in 2013.

A number of 2Tone bands re-formed in various incarnations, either as part of their original lineups or combined with members from other 2Tone bands. Noah Wildman, writing in his *People's Ska Annual* zine, claimed in the summer of 1996 that, "The new ska movement in the US has been chugging along nicely without the presence of 2Tone bands since the mid-eighties. Now that the ska scene is starting to eke its way into a broader consciousness in the US, Japan, South America and Australia, 2Tone bands are reforming to meet the demands of the markets that were not receptive to their wares the first time around. In other words: for the money" (p. 1). Wildman's comments about the revival were true, but his reasoning was suspicious, especially considering that fifteen years later he was taken to court on charges of embezzling thousands from Moon Ska Records, where he worked as storefront manager.

Other pioneers also went on tour to headline for modern acts, including Laurel Aitken, Derrick Morgan, Prince Buster, Toots & the Maytals, Justin Hinds, and Desmond Dekker. They all experienced a rebirth of their careers, through live performances, new recordings, and sales of their original recordings. Record labels began to reissue many out-of-print albums from decades earlier or put out collections of old material. In 1998, Island Jamaica Jazz released "Ball of Fire," a collection of many Skatalites tunes that were reworked, and most of their original work was released on CDs from a number of labels in a variety of compilations. Island Records released two fortieth anniversary collections featuring classic Jamaican ska from Prince Buster, Laurel Aitken, and dozens of others. Geffen Records released *Total Madness . . . the Very Best of Madness* in September 1997. Geffen also re-released much of The Specials' material, and Chrysalis re-released all of their singles as a collection in 1991. Re-releases were cheap to produce, were popular with audiences who craved the original sounds, and could sometimes mean money for the original artists through reworked deals that yielded royalties for the first time in their careers.

SKA BUST

It seemed ska had finally arrived in the United States, that it had finally achieved a similar status to ska in England and in Jamaica, although in a way that was uniquely American. New audiences had finally started to appreciate ska as a genre in its own right, rather than just as a precursor to reggae, and interpreted it in their own ways. So why did ska's popularity start to tank at the end of the 1990s?

To use a cliché, it was a perfect storm. First, the number of bands with the number of musicians in each band simply could not sustain themselves financially. As an example, if one venue that brought in a decent crowd of one or two thousand had to split the take of the door with five bands that each had five or ten members, each member would be lucky to get enough money to buy a beer, because the venue wasn't doling out that many free beverages. And this is assuming that band members were old enough to drink, which was another problem that venues had, making them less likely to book ska bands. Not all members were old enough to perform in many of the venues that booked ska bands: bars, or establishments with bars. All-ages shows were bad for bar tabs and therefore bad for venues. So when band members graduated from high school or college, they likely went off to other endeavors that were more lucrative than traveling around the country in a stinky van for twenty bucks a week.

Another factor that led to ska's decline was that compilations had watered down the market. They allowed ska fans to graze a little from each band, like on a buffet, but never really savor one band. Compilations made money for a label, which either split money among the bands on the album or paid each band a small flat fee to begin with. Either way, they weren't going to make much money for five to ten band members each, times ten bands on an album. The purpose behind a compilation was to introduce audiences to new bands. The rationale was that if they heard a band they loved, they would then go and seek the band's album. Many of these bands were so new that they had not produced an album yet, and many never recorded one because of a number of challenges too great to surmount. In addition, a kid with very little expendable income would have to truly love a band to shell out $15 for a CD. The chances that kids would hear a song on the CD that they loved so much as to compel them to buy an album were pretty good for the bands that were decent, but those were few and far between with the number of bands saturating the market, and only the decent bands retained their fans, with quality music. Having one good song did not mean that all a band's songs were great. Chances are the kids would just be satisfied with the compilation. So the odds were against the compilation working for most ska bands, and only the bands that were stellar could survive.

In a nutshell, there was oversaturation in the market. There were too many ska bands, with too many members, performing on too many compilations to promote tours that included too many bands on a bill. It was the very American tradition of overconsumption driven by capitalism. As Reel Big Fish sang in their song "Sell Out," which dealt with every ska band's dilemma of wanting success but not wanting to cheapen their art, no ska band members wanted to flip burgers for the rest of their lives, so there was nothing wrong with wanting to sign with a big label or have their albums be found in chain record stores across the country. It just so happened that there were thousands of similar-sounding characters with the same dream who tried to cash in on the same fifteen minutes of fame. Only the truly talented survived, if they were willing to stay in it for the long haul back to the underground. And that's right where many bands wanted to be. Lorraine Muller of Canadian band The Kingpins opined in 2000, "Did you watch the American Music Awards? My God, it made me sick. I'd really rather be part of something that the mainstream thinks is dead" (quoted in Lejtenyi 2000).

Bands started to be dropped from their big labels and began to break up—Fishbone, Hepcat, the Allstonians, the kick-ass Skoidats, Jump With Joey, to name a few. Others changed form. The Voodoo Glow Skulls focused more on their metal roots. No Doubt and the Mighty Mighty Bosstones stuck to their pop appeal, the former even producing teary-eyed ballads and hip-hop posturing. They no longer wanted to be classified as ska, although they said they had ska roots. "Ska is almost the marketing kiss of death," said Mikal Reich of Mephiskapheles. "We've been talking to record labels and they're always telling us they don't know how to market ska; they don't know who to sell it to. I used to think people in the record industry were barracudas and would jump on anything. Here you've got Rancid with a ska single in MTV's Buzz Bin and I still have to spell *ska* to people over the phone" (quoted in Strauss, 1997, p. 139).

Sire Records had sensed the American confusion over ska when marketing Madness to its U.S. market years earlier. People in the States just didn't get it. They didn't have the context that the West Indian immigrants provided in England, and they certainly didn't have the history that Jamaican society provided on the island itself. When distributing *One Step Beyond* in the United States, Sire sent out a press release stating, "To call Madness strictly a ska band is a mistake." The release contained a footnoted definition of ska to inform the reader, stating that it was "a pre-reggae form of Jamaican music, also known as bluebeat, skank and rocksteady." The release continued, "While most of their music has a definite rock steady beat, there's also a strong R&B and even straight rock edge to several of their songs." The American public probably was not familiar with the term rocksteady, but they knew rock, and wasn't that the same? Sire was banking on their making this assumption. The release concluded, "Music lovers coast-to-coast can discover the 'old' but incredible sound of bluebeat/R&B/rock performed by Madness." Ska was as confusing to marketers then as it is now.

What pushed ska out of what little radio rotation it had? Ska and the newest music on the radio did not share the same audience, but the bands were all vying for the same market share, the same record label contracts, and the same venue bookings, and boy bands like 'N Sync, 98°, and the Backstreet Boys took the stage. Heavier metal-based bands like Everclear, Evanescence, and Limp Bizkit; rap and soul artists like R. Kelly, Nelly, Outkast, Eminem, and Ludacris; and female vocalists capitalizing on the cliché that sex sells, like Britney Spears, Pink, and Destiny's Child, all became hits in the new millennium.

Ska seemed to become stale, especially when another genre of music was all the rage, ushering in clubs, fashion styles, and even classes at dance studios. The swing revival of the late 1990s stole some of ska's crossover audience, just as its popularity was waning. The swing revival was fueled by the popularity of the movie *Swingers*, which even featured Alex Désert of Hepcat in one of the main roles and included swing band Big Bad Voodoo Daddy in the sound track. The movie was cool and hip, and swing became all the rage. Swing was the centerpiece of a Gap commercial in 1998 in which swing dancers dressed in khakis did the Lindy hop to Louis Prima's "Jump, Jive, & Wail." Swing had hit the charts, including the Cherry Poppin' Daddies' "Zoot Suit Riot," Squirrel Nut Zippers' "Hell," and Big Bad Voodoo Daddy's "Go Daddy-O," which they performed during the 1999 Super Bowl half-time show on a football field full of swing dancers.

Another factor that contributed to ska's decline in the late 1990s was the demise of Moon Ska Records, the foundation and pillar of ska in the States. Shafer (2012) explains what transpired:

> Around late 97 early 98 there was a backlash against ska music and you'd see really snarky pieces on ska in *Billboard* and there were publications that said the next big thing was swing. A lot of the bands that major labels had presented as ska weren't really ska, so they weren't representative of the whole scene, like Smashmouth or Sugar Ray. There started to be backlash against them and it transferred to ska. Ska was being declared dead. There was a huge pushback. We started getting returns, massive returns from chains. We were used to loading up the UPS truck to ship out, but then all of a sudden the UPS guy started bringing back box after box of returns and it was horrifying. And it started accelerating. Pretty soon, chains just closed their whole ska section, and we owed the distributor money and bands weren't making anything and it was crushing. Several distribution companies were filing bankruptcy while owing Moon thousands of dollars in unpaid invoices, for albums that were already sent to stores. All of these factors led to the end of the Moon Ska store, and eventually, the label itself.

In addition, the manager of the Moon storefront, Noah Wildman, who had worked at Moon since 1995, was fired in 1999 for stealing nearly $100,000 in cash and an unknown additional amount in product, according to Bucket. The lack of revenue and stolen funds were devastating. Moon closed the label and storefront in 2000 for good. "Should there have been audits on the store? Sure, if you were looking at it from a business point of view, definitely, but it was just how the label was operated. I much preferred it that way and I don't think anyone should ever feel bad about it because it was amazing," says Shafer (2012), "but the writing was on the wall."

"By the late '90s ska was more successful than it was supposed to be," says Eric Rosen, a former A & R representative for Radical Records. "Ska is a very specific genre to be into, and when the major labels didn't want to buy it anymore, the distributors dropped it. Moon's mistake was in putting all its eggs in one basket, and when that basket is no longer attractive, you're in big trouble. They signed way too many bands and when it came crashing down it crashed really hard" (quoted in McLennan, 1998, p. C5).

Many of the Jamaican pioneers also stopped touring, due to either illness or death. Tommy McCook died in 1998 and had stopped touring with The Skatalites at least two years before. Roland Alphonso died shortly after McCook in 1998, after suffering from a burst blood vessel in his head while performing with The Skatalites onstage. Most of the 2Tone bands also stopped their revival touring, because their lineups changed with such regularity that continuity was virtually impossible, and original bandmates were too obstinate to reorganize. This removed a lot of the legitimacy and substance from the music. Ska became just a novelty act, silly and meaningless, especially as the country became more economically prosperous and the significance of the music was gone. Ska was relegated to children's cartoon theme songs and trite advertisement jingles.

Perhaps the most relevant factor, however, is that American ska frequently had little meaning, which is why it was susceptible to belittlement. An article that appeared in the *Chicago Tribune* in 1994, years before ska had fully realized its popularity and certainly before its demise in the States, had already noted the difference between American ska and its predecessor:

> There are those who think American ska needs a dose of social realism. That's what Pauline Black thinks, anyway. Black is the lead singer for The Selecter, one of the most political of the original English ska revival bands. While some of her contemporaries wrote odes to beer and shoplifting and the like, the Selecter and the Specials were composing anti-racist, anti-fascist anthems. "They're all very happy-go-lucky and 'let's have fun'," she says. "When The Selecter and The Specials came together, it was because we felt there were things that needed to be talked about." (Hockensmith, 1994, Tempo, p. 1)

This is not to say that British ska did not have its share of silliness, with songs like "Ne-Ne Na-Na Na-Na Nu-Nu" by Bad Manners or "Chipmunks Are Go!" by Madness, but there was still much being said as a whole by ska bands in Britain about unemployment, racism, and violence that communicated to those who identified with it and felt acknowledged by it. American ska in the '90s, with a few exceptions, was missing this social element. Instead, the bulk of American ska music was about futile topics like girlfriends, girlfriends with girlfriends, being a girl, beer beer beer, getting drunk, being cool, not eating pizza crust, how it sucks to be under twenty-one, Bumblebee Tuna, supporting your local ska band even though they stink, or are nerds, dorks, and midget pirates. Ska was always about uplifting the people's spirits, but ska in Jamaica had meaning—it carried the rhythms of the slaves, the horns of occupation, and the freedom from colonialism. Ska in England communicated love and unity in the face of rioting mobs of racists and discontented youths who had little hope for the future. In the United States, although some bands, like Fishbone and The Toasters, used the genre to be both lighthearted and serious about their culture, others were completely devoid of anything to communicate at all. Without the substance of lyrics, the music never went too deep, so it was easy to slough off.

Ska music also began to be consumed by the Internet, losing its innovation as the musical ear was swamped with too much information. Beverly Bryan, writing for MTV, says:

> In the 1980s and even in the 1990s, finding out about obscure musical forms required meeting people who were into the music, swapping rare imports with pen pals, and actually going to concerts. But, as music critic Simon Reynolds observes in his latest book *Retromania*, the Internet has got nearly everything archived, and that abundance of music's past is having an enormous impact on music's present. Reynolds fears this shift is retarding innovation. Retro movements have always existed, but Reynolds would say it's different this time because having access to countless pages of photographs, recordings, and footage takes all the conjecture and imagination out of that process. But maybe it's not all bad. Maybe this is a good time to look back and fully digest everything that has happened. (2010, mtviggy.com/articles/the-last-wave-why-ska-is-here-to-stay)

Scholar Joseph Heathcott reminds us that the success of ska in the States should be celebrated, and its hodgepodge of styles is a tribute to its roots: "We must not lose sight of the fact that ska constituted from its very beginnings a hybrid, transnational genre of music. Indeed, if we forget where ska comes from, how it evolved, and where it went, we forget that it was the music of working-class people in motion—not in stasis" (2003, p. 201). And ska is not in stasis: it is still evolving, still moving. Even though ska is no longer in the American mainstream, it endures underground, as well as all over the globe.

TEN

Ska All Over the World

To start off a chapter with the name "Ska All Over the World," especially in a book that has until now been fairly chronological in design, is, perhaps, misleading. One might think that it was only at this point, after developing in Jamaica in the 1950s and 1960s, moving overseas into England in the mid-1960s through the early 1980s, evolving into the U.S. from the early 1980s through the mid-1990s, that ska then spread to the world. This is not the case. Ska traveled to other parts of the world at various times over the decades as West Indians traveled and immigrated to countries near and far, as well as when tourists came to the islands from abroad. Similarly, the English version of ska also made the same leaps, like a seed carried by a finch across oceans, across land.

Ska has appeared in countries all over the globe and has blended with popular music of every sort to produce distinctive new varieties. Naturally, in the Latin American countries of Mexico, Central America, and South America, as well as in Spain and Cuba, Latin rhythms merged with the ska beat for a layered sound. In Asia, pop music and electronic affinities brought a novel approach to ska. In Africa, rhythm was king. And in Eastern and Western Europe, as well as in Australia, the 2Tone sound dominated. Through all interpretations of ska, however, one foot stayed firmly rooted in Jamaica, the land of ska's origin, whether overtly, as some bands tried and still try to continue in the tradition of its pioneers, or more subtly, to the point of blending in almost without detection.

WESTERN EUROPE

A review of ska in Western Europe starts with the mass immigration of West Indians in the 1960s, when skinhead reggae and blue beat evolved into 2Tone ska. But this wasn't the only outcome of ska in Europe. Bands like The Hotknives, Potato 5, The Burial, Gaz Mayall and His Trojans, and the all-female band The Deltones also came out of the United Kingdom during the 1980s, although they were never on the 2Tone label and are not necessarily associated with this sound. Unicorn Records was another ska label that helped sign many ska acts in England and throughout Europe, along with Gaz's Rockin' Records and Blue Beat Records, Buster Bloodvessel's label. Britain continued to produce ska bands in the years that followed, particularly Ska Cubano in 2002, who brought in a little Cuban flavor, reminiscent of Tommy McCook, Laurel Aitken, and Roland Alphonso. Also worthy of note are the female artists who brought 1960s soul into the new millennium and brought Jamaican ska with them. Amy Winehouse produced an EP of four songs of this era, including The Skatalites' song "You're Wondering Now" and the Toots & the Maytals song "Monkey Man," as well as The Specials' "Hey Little Rich Girl" and "Cupid" by Sam Cooke.

Italy's Vallanzaska formed in the mid-1990s, and their energetic sound was typical of the mid-1990s ska genre. Named after the notorious Italian mobster Renato Vallanzasca Costantini, their moniker lived up to the rudeboy/gangster tradition in ska. Perhaps one of the most popular ska bands in Spain, as well as worldwide, is Ska-P (pronounced "escape"). Part ska, part punk, this band formed in 1994 in Madrid and performed songs that addressed social and political concerns such as mestizaje, the Hispanic counterpart to creolization, the multiracial result of European colonization of the Latin people. Other songs dealt with child-molesting priests, pointing the finger directly at the pope for the cover-up; the wars between Palestine and Israel; animal experimentation in laboratories; religious laws on sexual freedom; and a society of consumption. Their sound may be more akin to punk and popular Hispanic music, but their strong horn section and lyrics full of social commentary are close to ska's roots.

Germany produced a great number of ska bands beginning in the 1980s, and its cities have been host to numerous widely attended ska festivals. The band Skaos formed in 1987 with an energetic 2Tone style. Skaos toured the United Kingdom with Bad Manners and acknowledged their Jamaican roots with an album called *Pocomania*. The Busters formed in 1987; in 1996 they achieved commercial recognition when they signed with Sony Records. Soon afterward, they established their own record label, in true ska tradition, called Revolution Records. They have toured with Jamaican pioneer Laurel Aitken and with fellow German ska artist Dr. Ring Ding. Although their lineup has changed many times over the years, they still perform, especially for German audiences.

Dr. Ring Ding himself is a German ska force. Since 1987, Richard Alexander Jung, who goes by his stage name Dr. Ring Ding, has performed trombone and been a vocalist in a number of bands and as a solo act. He started in El Bosso & die Ping Pongs before founding his own band, Dr. Ring-Ding & the Senior Allstars, in 1992, when he started to collaborate with Jamaican pioneers, including Lord Tanamo and Doreen Shaffer, both of The Skatalites. Over the years, he continued this tradition of collaboration with other artists, including Jamaicans Derrick Morgan, Hopeton Lewis, Phyllis Dillon, Bob Andy, Dennis Alcapone, as well as others, like The Toasters and even world boxing champion Sven Ottke.

In Holland, Def P & The Beatbusters began their foray into ska in the late 1990s with their blend of ska and hip-hop. Def P, also known as Pascal Griffoien, had done a previous stint as a rapper in Amsterdam, and his Dutch rhymes combine both the traditions of old school hip-hop and Jamaican toasting, backed by an ample horn section. Perhaps the most notable Dutch ska band, however, is Mr. Review. Founded in 1985, their debut album, *Walking Down Brentford Road*, paid homage to their Jamaican roots; Brentford Road is where Studio One is located in Kingston. Mr. Review released their most recent album in 2010.

In nearby Finland, the Valkyrians are considered the best-known ska band of their people and have won numerous national awards. This Helsinki group formed in the new millennium and recorded a number of cover songs, including Blondie's "Heart of Glass," Bob Marley's "Hooligan Ska," and "Ranking Full Stop" by The English Beat. Numerous other bands in Western Europe performed ska from time to time.

EASTERN EUROPE

Ska was even able to break through the Iron Curtain, proving that the music is stronger than any political or cultural boundaries. During the communist era, ska was able to seep in through, of all means, The Beatles. The Beatles were immensely popular in the Soviet Union in the 1960s, and their hit song "Ob-La-Di, Ob-La-Da" brought a Caribbean morsel to audiences there (although the song is most definitely not ska). The Beatles and other Western bands like The Rolling Stones, Deep Purple, and plenty of glam rock and heavy metal gained an underground popularity in the U.S.S.R., and Soviet bands that formed emulated this sound, although it was not recorded or distributed by the country's single label, Melodiya. Inspired by that Beatles tune, the first ska band to form in the Soviet Union was Strannye Igry from Leningrad, in 1982. The band, whose name is Russian for Strange Games, was founded by brothers Victor and Grigory Sologub. They performed ska along with punk for over a decade amid changing lineups. In 1989, the band Dva Samolyota, of Leningrad, also performed ska, albeit with more of a reggae and Afrobeat approach. In 1996, the band and its drummer, Mikhail Sindalovsky, founded the Griboyedov Club in the Ligovka area of what is now St. Petersburg, to support their own performances, as well as those of other local bands.

Ska gained further exposure in the Soviet Union with the tour of UB40 in 1986. This was the first time a Western band had been invited to perform anywhere in communist Eastern Europe, to "rock the bloc." Even though a security force was hired to prevent crowds from dancing at the series of concerts, the audiences were introduced to their first-ever live performance of ska and reggae. It was on many levels a groundbreaking event. The sound blew audiences away. As a result, many musicians went on to form their own bands, imitating the sound with horn sections and heavy rhythms.

After the dissolution of the Soviet Union in 1991, ska music in the countries formerly part of the U.S.S.R. gained freedom of expression. St. Petersburg became a hotbed for ska bands such as St. Petersburg Ska Jazz Review, Brosound, Banana Gang, Beshenye Ogurtsy, No Guns, and Porto Franco. None of these bands played in a style that one could confuse with the Jamaican pioneers. Their sounds were more ska punk and featured rapid-fire tempos. The rhythms certainly kept audiences dancing. Perhaps the two most popular ska bands to come out of Leningrad were Spitfire and Leningrad. Spitfire formed in 1993 in St. Petersburg and has since become one of the most notable ska bands from this city. With a distinctive mixture of ska and garage music, rockabilly, and punk, Spitfire have received exposure on numerous international compilations and have toured all over the world, including in the United States. Leningrad, founded in the late 1990s, are known for their obscene lyrics about women and vodka, as well as their combination of ska with rock and a Russian genre called chanson (originally called blatnaya pesnya), or songs with themes about the criminal world, not unlike the rudeboy and gangster themes in ska.

Ska has also prospered in other areas of the former Soviet Union. The group Kozhany Olen (K.O.) in the Ukraine began their ska core performances in 1998. Their vastly popular songs addressed cultural issues, such as AIDS, authority, and wars over oil. Perkalaba, also from the Ukraine, formed in 1998, blending the ska sound with punk and hutsul-folk native to the Carpathian mountain region. The list of ska bands from the former Soviet Union keeps growing, as the barriers to ska's sound have been torn down.

Elsewhere in Eastern Europe, ska is also popular and can vary in sound, unlike post-Soviet ska, which was mostly ska punk. In Budapest, Hungary, the Pannonia Allstars Ska Orchestra (PASO) began performing in 2003, with a sound reminiscent of the Jamaican originals. Lead vocalist Kristóf Tóth, who goes by the stage name Lord Panamo, dons a suit and hat for his performances in the tradition of Jamaican ska. Lyrics deal with the customary ska topics of condemning oppression and discrimination and encouraging tolerance. They have toured with American and European acts like The Toasters, NY Ska Jazz Ensemble, the Slackers, and Dr. Ring Ding, and they have been featured on the Megalith label.

In Poland, the ska band Vespa began performing in 1995. Many of their tunes feature female vocalist Alicja, who also performs on saxophone. Their song "Bujaj Się," translated as "swing out," is essentially a cover song of "Ghostbusters," but is popular with crowds and reminiscent of the 2Tone era. The song "To Miasto," Polish for "this is the city," is the "Free Bird" of every Vespa show and is a jazzy rocksteady number. Also hailing from Poland, Cala Gora Barwinkow (CGB) started in 2002 and are famous for their high-energy shows. Their sound is akin to The Toasters, so much so that only the Polish vocals will help the listener tell them apart. Their tight horns and strong skills have taken them to appearances at numerous music festivals and tours. The Polish band Skankan formed in 1993 and perform 2Tone-style ska. They have collaborated with numerous Polish musicians and performed at a multitude of concerts and on compilations.

In the former Yugoslavia, ska has become part of the repertoire of a band called Elvis Jackson of North Primorska, Slovenia. Formed in 1997, this band is a crazy blend of hard rock, punk, and ska. They have been commercially successful through collaborations with other international artists, record companies, and producers. They have toured all over the world and performed with such bands as Fishbone, The Toasters, The Offspring, Murphy's Law, Goldfinger, NOFX, and Ska-P.

MIDDLE EAST

Almost as surprising as ska's penetration through the Iron Curtain is its appearance in the Middle East. Dubai has been host to a number of Caribbean music festivals as West Indians have immigrated to the wealthy city. A Dubai band by the name of Gandhi's Cookbook was a rag-tag group of school chums who performed ska, along with hardcore punk, for about four years, and before breaking up they were able to tour India.

The band Beer7, hailing from Be'er Sheva (Hebrew for seven), Israel, performs a blend of ska and punk at clubs and concert halls throughout the country. Beer7 are more punk than ska, however, and they have written a song in tribute to Operation Ivy called "The Radio's Not a Friend," the video for which reached number one on the Israeli version of MTV, Music 24. Smash4$ is a band composed of Russian immigrants who speak Hebrew. They also play ska punk inspired by the Dropkick Murphys.

In Turkey, Athena is a ska punk band that began in 1987 with twin brothers Hakan and Gokhan Ozogua as a metal band. It wasn't until 1999 with their first album, *Holigan*, that they started playing ska and gained widespread popularity. In fact, the title song off that album became a hit in soccer stadiums. They have toured Turkey as well as internationally, performing with such bands as The Rolling Stones, the Pet Shop Boys,

Suede, Red Hot Chili Peppers, and Simple Minds. Their lyrics spoke out against the Iraqi War, and in 2005 they released an album of English-language songs. They perform regularly at soccer stadiums to soccer crowds. The Istanbul Ska Foundation, started in 2007, perform ska in the 2Tone tradition. Their sound is similar to the skinhead reggae that influenced the 2Tone bands, although they also perform plenty of jazz, swing, surf, hip-hop, raga, and Balkans music.

ASIA

It is not surprising that ska is big in Japan, as the cliché goes. It appears the Japanese have an affinity for all things Western. At the same time that ska became popular in the United States, during the 1980s and 1990s, it also experienced a boom in Japan. A group that is arguably the most popular is the Tokyo Ska Paradise Orchestra, which is now legendary. Founded in 1985, they have toured Europe more than six times and have played at well-known international music festivals. They have had commercial success and signed with Epic Records, producing eighteen studio albums over the course of many lineup changes. This immensely talented group has paid homage to ska's roots by covering a number of originals, such as The Skatalite's "Skaravan" at twice the original tempo, and the jazz standard "Wonderful World" by Louis Armstrong. In the tradition of showing affinity for cinema, they have recorded theme songs to the gangster classic *The Godfather* and the Japanese Bruce Lee classic *Enter the Dragon*.

Japan has a plethora of other ska bands, too numerous to list. Notable are OreSkaBand, who have also covered "What a Wonderful World." They are an all-female band that formed in 2003 when the members were only in middle school. They have performed with Jamaican legendary trombonist Rico Rodriguez and attracted record attendance at the prestigious Fuji Rock Festival before they had even graduated from high school. Shortly thereafter, they performed at the SXSW Festival in Austin, Texas, and toured with the Vans Warped Tour for two years. They signed with Sony Records. Yum! Yum! Orange, founded in 1999, has a sound akin to No Doubt, those pogo-inducing, chain-wallet-flinging rhythm bridges between ska refrains: pure pop. Perhaps their name, as well as the title of one of their albums, *Orange Street 33*, is a reference to Orange Street in Kingston, where Prince Buster and Leslie Kong had their record shops, and deejays like Tom "The Great" Sebastian played tunes, as well as to the number 33, the street address of the Treasure Isle recording studio, albeit on 33 Bond Street. Perhaps.

In China, communism prevented ska from gaining popularity, especially because live musical performances were restricted in number and location. Ska is by nature a live performance genre, so the limitations on concerts had an impact on its dissemination. Nevertheless, energetic, but not as silly as Japanese ska bands, Chinese ska bands like Toy Head from Beijing have been performing live since 2004 and even bring in the sounds of a flute from time to time. Others, like The K from central China, add a little rockabilly and punk to their ska. The K even had the honor of performing their takes of two Ramones' tracks for Marky Ramone when he visited in 2007 for the Beijing Pop Festival.

Perhaps most noteworthy of Chinese ska groups is the band The Trouble. Although they assembled as recently as 2010 in Chengdu in the Sichuan province of China, they perform traditional 1960s Jamaican ska, also performing songs that are ska punk with faster tempos. They have been equally influenced by The Skatalites and The Specials, and instruments appearing in their music include traditional horns as well as a violin and a hulusi, a Chinese flute-type instrument made with a gourd.

India's ska scene is almost nonexistent, save for a popular band from New Delhi called The Ska Vengers. Blending ska with jazz, dub, punk, and even rap, the group's male and female members tap into their affinity for Jamaica's Lee Scratch Perry and Marcia Griffiths, but also show respect for those like The Clash and The Velvet Underground. They performed at the Tihar Jail, which is the largest prison facility in south Asia, during an outdoor concert in the spring of 2012. Some 12,000 inmates were allowed to dance to ska, and the band donated a number of instruments to the prison's rehabilitative music program. Even in India, ska's connection to the underclasses is felt.

In Southeast Asia, Indonesia has an enormous ska scene with an indigenous feel that makes the music unlike any other. The golden age of ska in Indonesia was in 1999–2000, when ska music was seen as trendy and could be found in any number of cassette stalls in the country's shopping malls and markets, along with an ample supply of black and white checkered stickers, buttons, and other accessories. As a result, ska music was commercially successful, and large record labels signed many Indonesian ska bands like Tipe-X, Purpose, and Jun Fan Gung Foo. Most of these bands, however, were ska core like other bands in Asia, with energetic tempos, jackhammer drums, loud guitar, and pogoing crowds.

However, a number of ska bands combined ska with indigenous forms of Indonesian music and laid the foundation for ska that lasted beyond this boom. Ska blended with dangdut, a form of Hindi, Arab, and Malay musical styles. It is a popular dance music that incorporates vocals backed by a large number of musicians who perform on the tabla, or an Indian drum whose goat-skin membrane can be tuned using ropes on the sides; a kendung, or a two-headed large drum; and mandolins, guitars, and synthesizers. Dangdut is not unlike ska in many ways, so it is a natural fit for audiences who have an affinity for either style to acquire a taste for the other, and soon bands began to mix the two styles together, which became known as ska-duhut.

Another indigenous style that worked its way into the ska sound was jaipongan. When Indonesian president Sukarno banned Western music in 1961 and encouraged his people to create their own genres of music, dance, and other forms of art instead, jaipongan was created by Sudanese composer Gugum Gumbira for the Sudanese-speaking people of West Java. It was a dance form as well as a musical form; the two were intertwined. It uses multiple instruments, so it is no surprise that ska fused with jaipongan to create a hybrid called ska-pong. And in another region of Indonesia, the city of Cirebon in West Java, ska merged with the indigenous form of music, tarling Cirebonan, to produce ska-tarling. Ska became an ethnic form. The importance of these hybridizations is not only that ska was able to reach new audiences, but that the styles of the indigenous music came from the poor and working classes, the *orang kampung*, which was the same way that ska itself was formed.

AFRICA

The speed of Ska's dissemination into cultures and other genres in many lands was determined by politics and regimes, and countries in Africa were no exception to this rule. In South Africa, ska was fairly unknown until the 1990s, after apartheid had been eradicated as an oppressive and racist form of government. Since then, a handful of ska bands have emerged in the ska punk vein, including Hog Hoggidy Hog, Captain Stu, 7th Son, Little Kings, and The Rudimentals from Cape Town, and Fuzigish from Johannesburg. Many of these bands have had some success. Fuzigish supported the Violent Femmes in the late 1990s, and Hog Hoggidy Hog has opened for bands like NOFX and Mad Caddies. The Rudimentals, with a large horn section, stay closest to the original ska tradition, and perhaps even attempt to bring ska full circle, by combining ska with traditional African forms, both urban and rural. Their lyrics tackle issues close to many South Africans, such as AIDS, crime, and drug abuse.

Even though artist Baby Sol immigrated to the United Kingdom, her Congolese roots are strong, and she cross-pollinates reggae, dub, jazz, and ska. Most other countries on the continent of Africa have few or no ska bands to speak of, but plenty of reggae and certainly Afro-beat. Dub is also popular as electronic forms of music proliferate.

AUSTRALIA AND NEW ZEALAND

Once a commonwealth of Britain, Australia, not unlike Jamaica, has a shared cultural heritage with Great Britain. When ska came to England in the 1980s, it also came to Australia, and the bands that formed down under during these years had the same 2Tone sound. Bands included The

Jumpers from Adelaide; The Hangovers, Itchy Feet, Dr. Raju, and the Allniters from Sydney, as well as No Nonsense, The Letters, and perhaps the most popular of this era, Strange Tenants, from Melbourne. The Strange Tenants were founded in 1981 by brothers Ian and Bruce Hearn. Over the years, they have toured with big acts like UB40, Style Council, and U2, and in true 2Tone DIY tradition, they began their own record label, BlueBeat, on which they released their own work. Also like British ska bands, Strange Tenants brought political and social commentary to their music. Their songs spoke out against war and fascism, and their song "Hard Times" dealt with the issue of poverty in their city, not unlike Toots & the Maytals' "Time Tough" and countless other Jamaican ska tunes.

Australia's most popular band, The Porkers, began in 1987. Like much of the ska from the late 1980s and early 1990s worldwide, they produced a ska punk fusion. As a result, this music translated well to not only Australian crowds, but also American crowds, as The Porkers were distributed on Moon Ska Records in the mid-1990s.

Other bands that have come and gone and many that have remained in Australia include more in the ska punk genre, as well as some that play traditional jazz-based ska. The Melbourne Ska Orchestra are one such band. With over two dozen members on stage performing, with the front row seated and the back row standing, all behind music stands, their look is a combination of Tommy McCook meets Neville Staple. Their repertoire consists of many cover songs by The Skatalites, The Specials, and Madness, as well as originals.

Separated by just the Tasman Sea, New Zealand's ska scene was virtually the same as in Australia. A number of ska punk bands came from the island during the early to mid-1990s, such as Skapa, The Managers, The Screaming Orgasms, and The Offbeats. Battle-Ska Galactica was founded in 2009 in Wellington, with a mix of traditional Jamaican ska and 2Tone ska. The country is host to the annual Stony River Ska Festival, which brings in local ska bands from Wellington, Auckland, New Plymouth, and Tarnaki.

SOUTH AND CENTRAL AMERICA

Ska's appeal in Latin American cultures is massive, perhaps due in part to the origin of ska's rhythms, which come from the Caribbean via not only the African, but also the Spanish colonizers. In countries all over South and Central America, ska ensconces itself in other forms, like big band orchestras with multilayered compositions, as well as raw three-chord punk outfits playing two-and-a-half-minute sprints.

2Tone bands like Brazil's Skamoondongos, Sapo Banjo, Mr. Rude, and Skuba emerged in the late 1990s with a sound like that of the U.S. bands in the same era. Argentina's Los Calzones Rotos, who first performed live in Buenos Aires in 1988, also bring the 2Tone sound to Latin audiences, with plenty of peppy tempos and harmonizing horns, as well as the anthemic, bellowing, cerveza-swilling vocals that compel the audience to raise their cups and sing along. Other songs strayed into the punk-ska genre, like "Uno Dos Ultraviolento," a ska cover of Argentine-punk band Los Violidoras's classic song. Los Calzones Roto's video was shot inside cellblocks at Villa Devoto Prison, another nod to ska's association with the criminal element and underclasses. Perhaps Argentina's most successful band is Los Fabulosos Cadillacs, who took 2Tone in their own direction as they collaborated with artists like Debbie Harry, Mick Jones of The Clash, and Fishbone. They were nominated for Latin Grammy Awards and received numerous MTV Video Music Awards. They also had songs featured on sound tracks for movies like *Grosse Pointe Blank* and *Savages*. Also in Argentina, Sombrero Club stayed closer to the 2Tone roots, not only in their sound, heavy with punctuating keyboards, but in the content of their song lyrics as well: unemployment, depression, classism, and lack of opportunity for youth.

In Mexico in the mid-1980s, the tremendously popular rock band La Maldita Vecindad y los Hijos del Quinto Patio (which roughly translates to The Damn Housing Projects in English) brought ska into their repertoire and to the masses. Not only did they bring the ska sound to new audiences, but they also sang about social ills and disenfranchised youth. The effect of this was the creation of a number of ska bands in the 1990s and beyond, like Café Tacuba, who merged ska with pachanguera, or party music; La Matatena, who combined 2Tone with ska punk; Panteon Rococo with a myriad of ska styles; and countless others.

"Ska had been flourishing for a decade in Mexico and other parts of Latin America, with Mexican acts such as Panteón Rococó, Salon Victoria, and Tijuana No! becoming internationally recognized," writes Daniel Hernandez. "There, ska came to represent a movement of musical protest, just as it had during the second wave across England and the U.S., with bands often aligning themselves with social justice causes" (Hernandez, 2012, articles.latimes.com/2012/mar/18/entertainment/la-ca-latin-ska-20120318).

In Venezuela, Desorden Publico (Public Disorder) became one of the most notable ska bands to come out of Latin America. Formed in Caracas, Venezuela, in 1985, Desorden Publico was influenced by 2Tone bands and rose to superstar status, sharing the stage with such ska legends as Prince Buster, The Beat, Jerry Dammers, The Selecter, and King Chango, the New York band with Venezuelan roots. Also from Venezuela, Sin Sospechas began their 2Tone and ska punk days in 1989, encouraging others to form bands. Festivals and compilations followed.

Traditional ska bands cut from the same cloth as the Jamaican originals include Puerto Rico's La Fundación. This jazz-based band formed in late 1999; they have performed with The Skatalites, a perfect match, as well as New York's Stubborn All-Stars. In Mexico, this traditional ska merged with the mariachi band genre to produce a hybrid called Mexska, spawning bands like Los Matemáticos, Orquestra de Pablo Beltrán Ruíz, and musician Tono Quirazco as early as the 1960s. Quirazco performed many of Byron Lee's tunes, like "Jamaican Ska," although in Spanish, and he visited Kingston in 1965 to study the music that would become part of his catalog. He also added in a little Hawaiian guitar, not that distant in sound from the guitar of Jamaican Lyn Taitt. Mexico's El Gran Silencio took traditional ska and merged it with Jamaican forms like reggae, dancehall, and dub, but also with Latin forms like cumbia, vallenato, and banda. They became involved in a movement called Avanzada Regia, alternative music from Monterrey, Nuevo León.

Also combining traditional ska with Latin forms is Guatemalan band Malacates Trebol Shop, whose songs can range from ballads to pop. Peruvian band Vieja Skina has collaborated with many other traditional artists on their recordings, including Victor Rice of the New York Ska Jazz Ensemble and The Scofflaws, who produced Vieja Skina's album *Ayahuaska*. Ecuador's Sudakaya blends ska and reggae with ragamuffin and calypso, as well as samba and bossa nova.

The ska orchestra is almost a genre of its own, as the voluminous brass sections present in these conglomerations produce their own compositions. Orchestras had been popular in Latin and Central America, especially in Mexico, during the mid-1960s, as Tono Quirazco brought their sound to the Latin American people. It was a golden age. A few decades later, the genre is popular once again. Orquestra Brasileira de Música Jamaicana (OBMJ) formed in 2005. Their song list includes such ska classics as The Specials' "Ghost Town," as well as Brazilian classics like "The Girl from Ipanema." Their ska sambas, rocksteady, and dub have a distinctive Latin flavor, with extra percussion, like the guiro, cabasa, and cowbell. Formed in the same year, also from Brazil, the King Rassan Orchestra perform traditional 1960s Jamaican ska with samba and rumba. Included in their repertoire is everything from Duke Ellington to Cartola (samba master Angenor de Oliveira).

NORTH AMERICA

When ska music flourished in the United States in the mid-1990s, it was also popular in Canada. Montreal-based Stomp Records, like Moon Ska Records or Hellcat or Asian Man Records or Jump Up!, formed as a way to produce and distribute local ska bands. First releasing a compilation of these bands called *All Skanadian Club Vol. 1*, the label went on to release albums from The Planet Smashers, The Kingpins, The Undercovers, JFK & The Conspirators, Flashlight, Bedouin Soundclash, and Skavenjah.

The Planet Smashers performed in the ska punk genre, like most others of this era. One would be hard pressed, though, to argue that their lyrics were full of political and social content in the tradition of many Jamaican and British ska bands. Instead, The Planet Smashers wrote songs about peeing in elevators, getting drunk, getting pierced, hot girls, and orgies, but they did fulfill the mission of bringing good times to the crowd. They also brought back another tradition from the days of calypso—the art of innuendo.

King Apparatus were another Canadian ska band that had success, sticking close to their 2Tone roots. They had a hit song on Canadian radio stations in 1991 called "Made for TV," but their greatest success came from the solo work of King Apparatus's front man, Chris Murray. Murray moved to Los Angeles after the band broke up and recorded the now-classic solo album, *The Adventures of Venice Shoreline Chris*. Completely unembellished by production techniques, the album was recorded on a four-track cassette machine. It took much convincing to get Rob Hingley of Moon Ska Records to produce and distribute the album, but he finally did, and Murray even wrote and recorded a song about that experience, called "Cooper Station Blues."

Other popular Canadian ska bands include The Villains, who performed in the early to mid-1980s, The Afterbeat, The B-Sides, The Skanksters, General Rudie, Mad Bomber Society, Five Star Affair, and Tea for the Voyage, among others, all with sounds similar to U.S. bands of the same era.

After ska fell out of fashion in the United States and the chains had been removed from their wallets and Doc Martens put away, many bands continued on, and still others formed out of a passion for the music. Helping to breathe new life into these bands was Los Angeles band The Aggrolites, who coined the term for and performed a brand of ska called "dirty reggae." They formed in 2002 originally as studio musicians for Derrick Morgan, Prince Buster, Phyllis Dillon, and Culture's Joseph Hill. With one foot placed firmly in the roots of Jamaica, the other was planted in a harder, bellicose sound as they also performed backing instrumentals for Tim Armstrong of Rancid. They were just as much rock as they were rocksteady. Their song lyrics were about love and love loss, hard times and staying strong, and they wrote a song that captures the zeitgeist of Jamaican music in the new era, "Reggae Hit L.A."

The Aggrolites showed that respect for Jamaican roots was more than just in name. It wasn't enough to just say you were ska, or have a horn or two or play a syncopated beat. The Aggrolites demanded that their Jamaican forefathers be acknowledged properly. They introduced ska to the next generation by performing songs ("Banana," "Look Both Ways," "Animal Sounds," and "New Cats") for *Yo Gabba Gabba!*, the children's show on the Nick Jr. network. This show had a ska connection, as two of the program's creators were members of the popular 1990s ska band The Aquabats.

The Aggrolites didn't just introduce toddlers and preschoolers to ska, they also schooled the next generation of ska bands who returned to the rocksteady and skinhead reggae sound. The Green Room Rockers of Lafayette, Indiana, formed in 2006, had strong, soulful, raspy vocals and Hammond-organ-like keyboards by leader Mark Cooper. Their original compositions are reminiscent of Otis Redding and rocksteady greats like Alton Ellis, Toots Hibbert, and Stranger Cole. Their debut album, *Hoosier Homegrown*, was produced by The Slackers' Dave Hillyard, and they have performed with numerous original Jamaican artists. The Prizefighters of Minneapolis, formed in 2006, have also returned to Jamaican roots with their ska, rocksteady, and reggae originals. They have performed onstage with the Aggrolites, as well as pioneers like Stranger Cole, and their album, *Follow My Sound*, was mastered by world-renowned reggae producer King Django.

This is not to say that there are no bands in the United States in the new millennium that are still playing the ska punk of the previous era, like Streetlight Manifesto, who play NOFX and The Dead Milkmen cover songs and have machine-gun-fast tempos, but there is a resurgence of Jamaican-inspired bands that truly delve deep into catalogs and rare vinyl collections for their inspiration. Others in this vein include The Dropsteppers from Minneapolis and The Soul Radics from Nashville, who play alongside Jamaican pioneers (those who are still well enough to tour), as well as ska bands that refuse to die, like The Toasters, The Slackers, and Fishbone.

It is important to note that the ska model has changed, as have other forms of music in the United States and around the world, which brings ska full circle, in a way. Music today is purchased by the song, the mp3, like the 45, instead of an entire album. Hingley of The Toasters explains, "It's ironic that the music model for 2012 has reverted to what it was in 1962. I think now the concept of an album is something kids fail to grasp. I have 14 year old daughters and I was telling them about the concept of an album and they just couldn't wrap their heads around the thought of it. They download singles directly to their phone so the idea of going to a record store and buying an album is kind of beyond them. Things have very much reverted back to the '60s single driven model. In a way that's not so bad because it forces people to write good tunes" (Lawton 2012). Today, Hingley runs his successful Megalith label from his home in Spain.

JAMAICA

With such popularity worldwide, and such an authentic view of ska in the United States, ska has returned to its roots in many ways. It has gone all over the world, blended with every imaginable genre and influence, and come back to echo the same sounds and spirit. But in Jamaica, the country where it all started, few youths even know what ska is. Ask a kid on the streets of Kingston, a kid who may even be standing on an iconic street like Brentford Road or Orange Street, what ska is, and you are likely to either get a funny look or be told that it's "granny music" or the "oldies." Still, there are those in Jamaica who have made it their life's mission to preserve this history, like Herbie Miller, curator and founder of the Jamaica Music Museum; and Bunny Goodison, musicologist; Sparrow Martin, bandleader at Alpha Boys School, who trains the next generation of musicians; the university and scholarly publications that shed new light on old musicians; Stranger Cole, Doreen Shaffer, and Lester Sterling, who continue to tour, and those who toured until the day they died.

Ska may live abroad these days as Jamaican youths turn to dancehall for their entertainment and release. Large live bands rarely perform in Jamaica now; instead, electronic forms, easily portable, like the sound system once was, are found at every bashment. But ska cannot, like reggae, be relegated to a tempo button on a Casio keyboard and set up at every poolside bar on the island to provide background music for tourists. Nor can it be put on every beer can huggie or lighter or keychain or rearview mirror tchotchke like Bob Marley's face. Instead, ska requires a sizeable horn section, talent, and knowledge of jazz and calypso and mento and burru and call-and-response.

But the world is a different place than it was when the burru hid in the hills after slavery was abolished. It's a different place from the streets of Coventry or Brixton, where rioters expressed their anger at Thatcher and her policies. It's a different place than the graffiti-sprayed subways of New York City. And so ska enters a new dominion that knows no boundaries. It is no longer Jamaican, no longer British, no longer American or Mexican or Indonesian. It is the people's music. As Beverly Bryan writes:

> The ease of discovering music on the Internet may be helping to move ska out of the realm of periodically revived oddity, and, hopefully, move Jamaican music out of that silly "world music" file under. Nothing is obscure now. Or at least nothing seems to stay obscure for long. When you can hear whatever you want with one click and then read about it just as quickly, it actually gets easier to place music in context—and incorporate musical ideas into your own creative process. That's why, while there doesn't seem to be another wave on the horizon, this generation's discovery of ska may be just beginning. And

surely it's just a small part of something much larger (2010, mtviggy.com/articles/the-last-wave-why-ska-is-here-to-stay/).

Ska has always been the people's music. Whether it is received on the street corner, in a concert arena, or through earphones, ska is still the people's music, in whatever form it takes.

References and Further Reading

"After a Wild Week on Wall Steet, the World Is Different." *Time*, November 2, 1987.

Aitken, Laurel. Interview with the author, July 6, 1997.

Alphonso, Roland. Interview with the author. May 17, 1997.

Augustyn, Heather. 2010. *Ska: An Oral History*. Jefferson, NC: McFarland. With a foreword by Cedella Marley telling of her father's start in ska, this book includes words from over thirty-five legends of ska—Jamaican, British, and American pioneers.

Barrett, Leonard. 1976. *The Sun and the Drum*. Kingston, Jamaica: Sangster's Book Stores.

———. 1997. *The Rastafarians*. Boston: Beacon Press, 1997. A classic history of the Rastafarian movement in Jamaica, from Paul Bogle to Back-O-Wall. Exceptional coverage of the rise of Ethiopianism and its connection to Rastafarianism.

Barrow, Steve. 1993. "Tougher Than Tough: The Story of Jamaican Music" [CD booklet]. London: Mango Records.

———. 1998. "Ska Boo-Da-Ba. Top Sounds from Top Deck" [CD booklet]. London: Westside.

———, and Peter Dalton. 1997. *Reggae: The Rough Guide*. London: Rough Guides.

Bedway, Yvette. 1965. "Too Much Ska." *The Daily Gleaner*, November 21, p. 12.

BGSU Lib Guides. n.d. "Ska." http://libguides.bgsu.edu/content.php?pid=46362&sid=344662 (accessed March 27, 2013).

Black, Pauline. Interview with the author. November 14, 2007.

———. 2011. *Black by Design: A 2-Tone Memoir*. London: Serpent's Tail. A fascinating biography written with all of the charisma and personality of this vivacious artist.

Brackett, Nathan and Christian Hoard (2004). *The New Rolling Stone Album Guide*. New York: Simon & Schuster, p. 298.

Bradley, Lloyd. 2000a. *Bass Culture: When Reggae Was King*. London: Penguin Books.

———. 2000b. *This Is Reggae Music: The Story of Jamaica's Music*. New York: Grove Press. A thorough account of the rise of Jamaican music from the early days, with excellent detail and words from artists both familiar and obscure. Perhaps the most comprehensive version of the sound system era, the significance of their existence, and the contribution they made to setting the foundation upon which Jamaican music was built.

Brevett, Lloyd. Interview with the author, May 17, 1997.

Bryan, Beverly. 2011. "The Fourth Wave: Is Ska Finally Here to Stay?" *MTV Iggy*, October 5, mtviggy.com/articles/the-last-wave-why-ska-is-here-to-stay (accessed June 30, 2013).

Bushell, Garry. "Rude Boys Can't Fail." *Sounds*. March 15, 1980.

Chang, Jeff. 2005. *Can't Stop Won't Stop: A History of the Hip-Hop Generation*. New York: Picador, 2005.

Clarke, Sebastian. 1980. *Jah Music: The Evolution of the Popular Jamaican Song*. London: Heinemann Educational Books.

Cooke, Mel. 2013. "Hague, Miller Locate Jamaica in jazz—Perceptions of Being an Elitist Music Form Refuted." *Daily Gleaner*, February 23, p. Entertainment 1.

Cowley, John. 1996. *Carnival, Canboulay, and Calypso: Traditions in the Making*. Cambridge, UK: Cambridge University Press.

DeLisser, Herbert G. 1910. *In Jamaica and Cuba*. Kingston, Jamaica: The Gleaner Company.

Derbyshire, J. Denis, and Ian Derbyshire. 1990. *Politics in Britain from Callaghan to Thatcher*. New York: W. & R. Chambers Ltd..

Du Noyer, Paul. 1981. "Giving Up the Ghost?" *New Musical Express*, August 8, pp. 18–19.

Ellis, Trey. 1989. "The New Black Aesthetic." *Callaloo*. (Winter): pp. 233–243.

Erlewine, Stephen Thomas. Fishbone. thebossbookingagency.com/fishbone

Foehr, Stephen. 2000. *Jamaican Warriors: Reggae, Roots & Culture*. London: Sanctuary Publishing.

Foster, Chuck. 1999. *Roots Rock Reggae: An Oral History of Reggae Music from Ska to Dancehall*. New York: Billboard Books.

———. 2009. *The Small Axe Guide to Rock Steady*. London: Muzik Tree & I Am the Gorgon.

Goodall, Graeme. 2011. Interview with author, July 13.

———. 2013. Interview with author, February 8.

Gordon, Shirley. 1983. *Caribbean Generations*. London: Longman Group Ltd.

Halasa, Malu. 1981. *The Beat: Twist and Crawl*. Richmond, UK: Eel Pie Publishing.

Hall, Stuart, and Tony Jefferson. 2000. *Resistance Through Rituals: Youth Subcultures in Post-war Britain*. New York: Routledge.

Heathcott, Joseph. 2003. "Urban Spaces and Working-Class Expressions across the Black Atlantic: Tracing the Routes of Ska." *Radical History Review* (Fall): pp. 183–206.

Hebdige, Dick. 1987. *Cut 'N' Mix: Culture, Identity and Caribbean Music*. London: Comedia. Essential information on how the European and African traditions of the Caribbean combined to create the environment for ska and reggae, as well as some information on the move to England and a decent section on the emergence of hip-hop.

Hernandez, Daniel. 2012. "A New Wave of Rude Boys on SoCal Dance Floors." *Los Angeles Times*, March 18, articles.latimes.com/2012/mar/18/entertainment/la-ca-lat-in-ska-20120318.

Hill, Errol. 1971. "Calypso." *Jamaica Journal*, Vol. 5, No. 1, pp. 23–27.

Hockensmith, Steve. 1994. "The Return Of Ska: Young Bands, Young Audiences Bring Back Reggae's Lively Ancestor." *Chicago Tribune*, October 7, Tempo p. 1.

Honeysett, Laurence, and Michael de Koningh. 2003. *Young, Gifted and Black: The Story of Trojan Records*. London: Sanctuary.

"Hotel Flamingo" advertisement. 1962. *The Daily Gleaner*, August 3, p. 6.

Hutton, Clinton. 2007. "Forging Identity and Community Through Aestheticism and Entertainment: The Sound System and the Rise of the DJ." *Caribbean Quarterly* (December): pp. 16–31.

———. 2010. "Oh Rudie: Jamaican Popular Music and the Narrative of Urban Badness in the Making of Postcolonial Society." *Caribbean Quarterly* (December): 22.

Hylton, Patrick. 1975. "The Politics of Caribbean Music." *The Black Scholar* (September): pp. 23–29.

"Independence Showcase" advertisement. 1962. *The Daily Gleaner*, August 3, p. 6.

Isler, Scott. 1993. "2 Tone: A Checkered Past" [CD booklet]. London: Chrysalis Records.

"Jamaica Festival" advertisement. 1964. *The Daily Gleaner*, July 25, p. 19.

"Jamaican Life Will Be Shown in Dance." *The Daily Gleaner*, July 19, p. 2.

Jones, J. R. 1998. "Ska's Lost Cause." *Chicago Reader*, July 23, chicagoreader.com/chicago/skas-lost-cause/content?oid=896881 (accessed June 30, 2013).

Katz, David. 2003. *Solid Foundation: An Oral History of Reggae*. New York: Bloomsbury. A comprehensive oral history of reggae, with ample attention given to the early years, from a masterful writer. Also includes a nice selection of photos and first-hand memories of the sound system days. The number of artists interviewed reaches into the triple digits.

———. 2004. "Ken Khouri: I Am the Complete Pioneer of Everything." *Caribbean Beat Magazine* 67 (May/June): caribbean-beat.com/issue-67/ken-khouri-%E2%80%9Ci-am-complete-pioneer-everything%E2%80%9D.

Keyo, Brian. 1996. "Foundation Ska: A Brief History of the Skatalites" [CD booklet]. Cambridge, Massachusetts: Heartbeat Records.

Knibb, Lloyd. Interview with the author. May 17, 1997.

Kong, Dr. Basil Waine. 2009. "Racism and Classism in Jamaica." Jamaicachapter, July 6. jamaicachapter.blogspot.com/2009/07/racism-and-classism-in-jamaica.html (accessed July 26, 2013).

Kot, Greg. 1997. "Ska Ska Ska: Underground Sound Wave Crashes Top of Charts." *Chicago Tribune*, July 17, Tempo p. 1.

Lawton, Adam. 2012. "Interview with Robert 'Bucket' Hingley." *Media Mikes*, February 22. http://www.mediamikes.com/2012/02/interview-with-robert-hingley/ (accessed March 27, 2013).

"Learning to Dance . . . !" 1964. *New York Amsterdam News*, May 2, p. 1.

Lee, Helene. 2004. *The First Rasta: Leonard Howell and the Rise of Rastafarianism*. Chicago: Chicago Review Press. Lee follows the events of Leonard Howell's past like a detective, tracing the roots of the rise of Rastafarianism.

Lejtenyi, Patrick. 2000. "Ska-Boom and Ska-Bust." *Exclaim.ca* (February). http://exclaim.ca/Features/Research/ska-boom_ska-bust (accessed March 27, 2013).

Lowe, Agatha. 1995. "Themes of War, Politics, and Health Education in Calypso Music." *Caribbean Quarterly*, Monograph, pp. 56–72.

Malcolm, Carlos. 2011. Interview with author, December 26.

Marshall, George. 1994. *Spirit of '69: A Skinhead Bible*. Scotland: S.T. Publishing.

McLennan, Scott. 1998. "Hepcat Heavy into Reggae-ska Revival." *Telegram & Gazette*, February 17, p. C5.

Miles, Barry. 1981. *The 2-Tone Book for Rude Boys*. London: Omnibus Press.

Millar, Robbi. 1981. "No Surrender to Racism!" *Sounds*, January 17, pp. 32–33.

Miller, Herbie. 2007a. "Brown Girl in the Ring: Margarita and Malungu." *Caribbean Quarterly* (December): 47–74. This article is essential reading for anyone wanting to know more about the legendary trombonist Don Drummond and Anita Mahfood. Miller mixes historical fact that he has uncovered through his long-time research into the subject with his critical analysis of the events to produce an indispensable account of the importance of these two tragic figures.

———. 2007b."Don Drummond, Jazz and Black Nationalism." *Jamaica Observer*, May 23, pp. 26–27.

Mills, Claude. 1998. "Lord Creator Has a Passion for Ballads." *The Sunday Gleaner*, April 12, p. 3E.

Mohair Slim. n.d. "The Untold Story of Jamaican Popular Music." Reproduced in a discussion board post at Dancehallreggae.com (accessed August 10, 2007).

Morgan, Derrick. 1997. Interview with author, June 5.

"MTV Changed the Music Industry on August 1, 1981." 1998. *CNN & Entertainment Weekly Report*, July 31. www.cnn.com/SHOWBIZ/Music/9807/31/encore.mtv/index.html?_s=PM:SHOWBIZ (accessed March 28, 2013).

"Myrtle Bank Hotel Announces Its Independence Programme." 1962. *The Daily Gleaner*, August 3, p. 6.

Niaah, Sonjah Stanley. 2005/2006. "Kingston's Dancehall Spaces." *Jamaica Journal* 29 (December–April): 3, pp. 14–33.

Nickson, Chris. 1997. "Ska's Checkered Past." *Alternative Press* (March): pp. 31–34.

Nunley, John, and Judith Bettelheim. 1988. *Caribbean Festival Arts*. Seattle: University of Washington Press.

O'Brien Chang, Kevin, and Wayne Chen. 1998. *Reggae Routes: The Story of Jamaican Music*. Philadelphia: Temple University Press.

"Photo Stand alone." 1964. *New York Amsterdam News*, August 29, p. 16.

Porter, Christopher. 2004. "Jazz to Ska Mania." July/Aug. jazztimes.com/articles/14829-jazz-to-ska-mania (accessed June 29, 2013).

Potash, Chris. 1997. *Reggae, Rasta, Revolution: Jamaican Music from Ska to Dub*. New York: Schirmer Books. A collection of essays written by various authors about various eras of Jamaican music and the forms that subsequently evolved.

Pouchet Paquet, Sandra, Patricia Saunders, and Stephen Steumpfle. 2007. *Music Memory Resistance: Calypso and the Caribbean Literary Imagination*. Kingston, Jamaica: Ian Randle Publishers.

Rambali, Paul. 1980. "The Promised Land Calling." *New Musical Express*, February 9. pp. 30–33.

Reckord, Verena. 1982. "Reggae, Rastafarianism and Cultural Identity." *Jamaica Journal* (August): pp. 71–79.

Regis, Louis. 1999. *The Political Calypso: True Opposition in Trinidad and Tobago 1962–1987*. Gainesville: The University Press of Florida.

Robinson, Greg. 1997. "The Skatalites: Playing the Jamaican Sound." *Windplayer*, no. 51, pp. 14–23.

Staple, Neville, and Tony McMahon. 2009. *Original Rude Boy*. London: Aurum Press Ltd.

Sterling, Lester. Interview with the author, May 17, 1997.

Seaga, Edward. 2012. "From Colony to Independence, Pt. 1." *Jamaica Gleaner*, July 15, jamaica-gleaner.com/gleaner/20120715/focus/focus.html (accessed June 26, 2013).

Sealy, Theodore. 1962. "Independence—How to Celebrate It!" *Sunday Gleaner*, February 18, p. 6.

Shafer, Steve. Interview with author, September 9, 2012.

Shaffer, Doreen. Interview with author, May 17, 1997.

Stone, Carl. 1973. *Class, Race, and Political Behaviour in Urban Jamaica*. Institute of Social and Economic Research, University of the West Indies, Jamaica.

Stratton, Jon (2010). "Chris Blackwell and 'My Boy Lollipop:' Ska, Race, and British Popular Music." *Journal of Popular Music Studies* 22, no. 4: pp. 436–465.

Strauss, Neil. 1995. "The Sound of New York: Ska. Ska? Yes, Ska." In Chris Potash (ed.), *Reggae, Rasta, Revolution*. New York: Schirmer Books, pp. 136–139.

Strong, William. 1964. "You Can Quote Me . . . ." *The Daily Gleaner*, August 10, p. 10.

"Take Jamaica Home with you!" advertisement. 1966. *The Daily Gleaner*, August 13, p. 10.

Taitt, Lyn. 2009. Interview with author, June 11.

Tanna, Laura. 1984. *Jamaican Folk Tales and Oral Histories*. Kingston, Jamaica: Institute of Jamaica Publications Ltd.

Thompson, Dave. 2004. *Wheels Out of Gear: 2Tone, The Specials, and a World in Flame*. London: Helter Skelter Publishing.

"TV Interview for Granada World in Action." Margaret Thatcher Foundation. January 27, 1978. margaretthatcher.org/document/103485 (accessed July 29, 2013).

Usamanont, Frank. 2009. "The Birth of the 1980's NYC Ska Scene—Beat Brigade." May 30. marcoonthebass.blogspot.com/search?q=beat+brigade (accessed March 29, 2013).

White, Cathy. 1964. "Personally and Socially: The Jamaica Ska Takes Over!" *New York Amsterdam News*, May 30, p. 18.

White, Garth. 1967. "Rudie, Oh Rudie!" *Caribbean Quarterly* (September): 39.

_____. 1986. "Patriarchs of Sound: Popular Music's Early Instrumentalists." *The Jamaican* (December): 39–40.

_____. 2007. "Social and Aesthetic: Roots of Ska." *Caribbean Quarterly* (December): 53, no. 4 (2007): pp. 80–95.

White, Timothy. 1983. *Catch a Fire*. New York: Henry Holt. Perhaps the best account of Marley's life, and perhaps one of the best biographies ever written. Marley's life is told in a narrative style that makes the details and morsels stimulating.

"Why 492 West Indians Came to Britain." 1948. *Guardian*, June 23. century.guardian.co.uk/1940-1949/Story/0,,105104,00.html (accessed July 29, 2013).

Wildman, Noah. 1996. "2Tone Today: Prime Rib or Spam?" *The People's Ska Annual* (Summer): pp. 1–2.

Williams, Mark. 2006. "Alpha Boys' School: Music in Education" [CD booklet]. London: Trojan.

Williams, Paul. 1995. *You're Wondering Now: A History of The Specials*. Scotland: S.T. Publishing.

Wilson, Ainsley. 1964. "The Ska." *The Daily Gleaner*, April 16, p. 10 .

Wilson, Chris. 2006. *Bonanza Ska: The Studio One Years* [Liner notes]. Heartbeat Records.

Further Listening

DVDS

Bad Manners: Don't Knock the Bald Heads. Directed by Dave Meehan. Pottstown, PA: Mvd Visual, 2005.

Dance Craze. Directed by Joe Massot. London: Osiris Films, 1981.

Duke Vin and the Birth of Ska. Directed by Gus Berger. Melbourne: Gusto Films, 2008.

English Beat — In Concert at the Royal Festival Hall. Directed by Dave Meehan. Milwaukee, WI: Hal Leonard Publishing, 2005

Everyday Sunshine: The Story of Fishbone. Directed by Chris Metzler and Lev Anderson. New York: Cinema Guild, 2012.

The First Rasta (le Premier Rasta). Directed by Hélène Lee. Paris: Kidam, 2010.

The Harder They Come. Directed by Perry Henzell. New York: Criterion, 2000.

Laurel Aitken and Friends, Live at Club Ska. London: Cherry Red UK, 2005.

Quadrophenia. Directed by Franc Roddam. New York: Criterion, 2012.

Rocksteady: The Roots of Reggae. Directed by Stascha Bader. Studio City, CA: Lightyear Entertainment, 2010.

The Selecter: Live from London. Directed by Dave Meehan. Pottstown, PA: Mvd Visual, 2005.

Ska Explosion. London: Cherry Red UK, 2004.

CDS

Count Ossie and The Mystic Revelation of Rastafari. *The Spiritual Roots of Reggae: The Original Complete Grounation.* Ravenna: Déjà Vu Italy, 2007. The Burru drumming of Count Ossie's group is essential listening to see how these rhythms became part of the repertoire. A two-disc set.

The English Beat. *Just Can't Stop It.* Los Angeles: Shout Factory!, 2012. Many of the band's best tunes, including "Mirror in the Bathroom," "Ranking Full Stop," and "Tears of a Clown."

Fishbone. *The Essential Fishbone.* New York: Sony, 2003. Fantastic selection including "Party at Ground Zero," "Skankin' to the Beat," and "Freddie's Dead."

Madness. *One Step Beyond.* London: Salvo, 2009. An outstanding two-disc collection of their debut album, including a disc of Peel Session versions.

The Selecter. *Greatest Hits.* Hollywood, CA: Emd Int'l (Capitol Records), 1996. All of the best tunes are here, including, "On My Radio," "Three Minute Hero," and "Too Much Pressure."

The Skatalites. *Anthology.* Marlow, UK: Culture Press, 2007. A two-disc set of thirty-five songs with all of the classics. Essential listening.

The Skatalites. *Foundation Ska.* Cambridge, MA: Heartbeat, 1997. Another essential collection of The Skatalites' greatest tunes in this two-disc set, including Margarita's "Woman A Come." Worth the buy just for the liner notes alone, which are substantial.

The Skatalites. *Ska-Boo-Da-Ba: Top Sounds from Top Deck, Volume Three.* London: Westside Records UK, 1998. All Skatalites tunes, recorded by Justin Yap during an all-night session.

The Specials. *Specials*. Hollywood, CA: Capitol Records, 2002. A collection of their best hits, remastered.

The Toasters. *30th Anniversary*. London: Phoenix City Records, 2012. This disc contains twenty of the band's best from their long career, including a live version of "Matt Davis."

Tokyo Ska Paradise Orchestra. *Paradise Blue*. Tokyo: AVEX Entertainment, 2010. A nice two-disc selection of tight horns from this massive Japanese ska band.

Various Artists. *Alpha Boys ' School: Music in Education*. London: Trojan Records, 2006. This twenty-three-song collection of Alpharians demonstrates how ska evolved from jazz with selections from Joe Harriott and Dizzy Reece as well as Rico Rodriguez, Vin Gordon, Lester Sterling, Don Drummond, and others. Substantive liner notes as well.

Various Artists. *Folk Music of Jamaica*. Washington, DC: Smithsonian Folkways Archival, 2007. Edward Seaga's collection of work from 1956, including Kumina, Zion, and Pukkumina music. Hear work songs, ring play, and spirituals.

Various Artists. *The Historic Roots of Ska*. Marlow, UK: Culture Press, 2007. A two-disc set featuring The Skatalites, Duke Reid, Toots & the Maytals, Baba Brooks, and many other early artists. A nice sample of the early years.

Various Artists. *Ska Bonanza: The Studio One Ska Years*. Cambridge, MA: Heartbeat, 2000. A two-disc set featuring classics from The Skatalites, Stranger Cole, Toots & the Maytals, and early Wailers.

Various Artists. *Ska-Ta-Shot: Top Sounds from Top Deck, Volume Four*. London: Westside Records UK, 1998. Features a number of artists who recorded for Justin Yap, including solo work by The Skatalites' Johnny Moore, Roland Alphonso, and Jackie Mittoo, along with the title track by Lynn Taitt.

Various Artists. *This Are Moon Ska: Vol. 2*. New York: Moon Ska Records, 1997. A good sampling from the likes of The Toasters, The Skoidats, Skinnerbox, Let's Go Bowling, The Scofflaws, and many others.

Various Artists. *Treasure Isle Records Presents Ska: 1966 to 1968*. London: Spectrum Music, 2012. A two-disc collection of forty songs from Duke Reid's Treasure Isle label that demonstrates how ska evolved into rocksteady.

Various Artists. *The Two Tone Collection: A Checkered Past*. London: Chrysalis Records, 1993. Essential listening for the British era of ska with classics from The Specials, The Selecter, The Beat, Madness, and others. Two discs comprise forty-four songs and nice liner notes.

Index

155

About the Author

Heather Augustyn is a journalist and writing teacher living in Chesterton, Indiana, one hour outside of Chicago. She author of *Ska: An Oral History* (2010), with a foreword by Cedella Marley, which was nominated for the ARSC Award for Excellence, and *Don Drummond: The Genius and Tragedy of the World's Greatest Trombonist* (2013), with a foreword by Delfeayo, Marsalis.

Feature articles on Augustyn's work have appeared in the *Jamaica Gleaner*, *Jamaica Observer*, and *The Onion's A/V Club* among dozens of others. She has been co-host of *Radio M* on WBEZ-FM, Chicago's NPR station with Tony Sarabia, spoke on NPR's *Sound Opinions*, and was interviewed for radio shows in Indiana and Minneapolis. She is a great fan of ska, rocksteady, and reggae music and has been invited to lecture at the International Reggae Conference in Kingston, Jamaica, where she spoke on women in ska and music of Jamaican independence. She is currently serving as an assistant director for a documentary, *Man in the Street*, based on the life of Don Drummond from Gusto Films in Melbourne.

Augustyn has been a correspondent for *The Times of Northwest Indiana*, the state's second-largest newspaper, since December 2004. She is contributing editor for *Shore Magazine* and is managing editor of the quarterly *Duneland Today Magazine*. Her work has appeared in such national publications as *The Village Voice*, *The Humanist Magazine*, *World Watch Magazine*, *E! The Environmental Magazine*, and she was the last journalist to interview the late novelist Kurt Vonnegut. The story appeared in *In These Times Magazine* and was published in the book *Kurt Vonnegut: The Last Interview and Other Conversations*, Melville House, 2011.

Augustyn is also a professional photographer and her work has appeared in numerous magazines and books. She received her M.A. in writing from DePaul University and a B.A in English and philosophy from Bradley University. She currently directs a Montessori school's writing program in northwest Indiana, where she and her husband Ron have two boys, Sid and Frank.